Copy and Reference Puzzlers Book 2

128 FUN Puzzles

Jason Turner

Copy and Reference Puzzlers Book 2

128 FUN Puzzles

Jason Turner

ISBN 9798817267822

Also By Jason Turner

C++ Best Practices

Object Lifetime Puzzlers Book 1

Copy and Reference Puzzlers Book 1

Opcode Puzzlers Book 1

Object Lifetime Puzzlers Book 2

Copies and References

This puzzle book focuses on value copies and references. You'll have to trace what values change when a new value is assigned.

The goal of this puzzle book is to use as few words as possible. Instead you will learn how to do the puzzles simply by looking at examples.

Important note:

Anything starting with // is a "comment" and has no impact on the code!

A Note On Puzzle Layout

Some puzzles split across pages. Sometimes this is annoying. I've decided to leave it how it is because it adds a sense of realism to what it's actually like to read unnecessarily complex C++ code.

How C++ Relates

Each of these examples are real C++ code. If you are a C++ user, you can learn more about object lifetime with these puzzles.

Each solution is a topic that has something to do with C++. If you cannot figure out what the solution means, then duckduckgo for it and learn something new :).

If you aren't a C++ user then don't worry about any of this, just have fun!

About Jason Turner

Jason is a developer, speaker, and trainer who specializes in C++. His goal is to make C++ as approachable, fun, and accessible as possible. This book is part of that effort. Jason can be contacted via emptycrate.com. Be sure to check out his YouTube channel, "C++ Weekly."

Values

Value Example 1

```
void run()
{
  print("5");
}

// Answer: 5
```

Value Example 2

```
void run()
{
  print("{}", 5);
}

// Answer: 5
```

Value Example 3

```
int value()
{
  return 5;
}

void run()
{
  print("{}", value());
}

// Answer: 5
```

Value Example 4

```
void run()
{
  int value = 5;
  print("{}", value);
}

// Answer: 5
```

Value Example 5

```
void run()
{
  print("{}{}", 4, 2);
}

// Answer: 42
```

char Puzzles

Puzzle 1

```
void run() {
  char char_1{'q'};
  char_1 = 'c';
  char char_3{'h'};
  char_3 = 'y';
  char char_5{'p'};
  char_5 = 'l';
  char char_7{'t'};
  char_1 = 'f';
  char char_9{'r'};
  print("{}{}{}",
        char_7, char_9, char_5);
}

// Answer (3):

// __ __ __
```

Puzzle 2

```
void run() {
  char char_1{'h'};
  char_1 = 'm';
  char char_3{'q'};
  char_3 = 'o';
  char char_5{'h'};
  char_1 = 'r';
  char char_7{'v'};
  char_5 = 'i';
  char char_9{'s'};
  print("{}{}",
        char_5, char_9);
}

// Answer (2):

// __ __
```

Puzzle 3

```
void run() {
  char char_1{'m'};
  char_1 = 'p';
  char char_3{'o'};
  char_1 = 'x';
  char char_5{'S'};
  char_3 = 'n';
  char char_7{'R'};
  char_1 = 'h';
  char char_9{'X'};
  char_3 = 'A';
  char char_11{'k'};
  print("{}{}{}{}",
        char_5, char_3, char_7, char_9);
}

// Answer (4):

// __ __ __ __
```

Puzzle 4

```
void run() {
  char char_1{'a'};
  char_1 = 'b';
  char char_3{'u'};
  char_3 = 'c';
  char char_5{'u'};
  char_1 = 'n';
  char char_7{'o'};
  char_3 = 'v';
  char char_9{'t'};
  char_1 = 'r';
  char char_11{'b'};
  print("{}{}",
        char_7, char_1);
}

// Answer (2):

// __ __
```

Puzzle 5

```
void run() {
  char char_1{'d'};
  char_1 = 'i';
  char char_3{'y'};
  char_3 = 'd';
  char char_5{'j'};
  char_3 = 'u';
  char char_7{'l'};
  char_5 = 'c';
  char char_9{'a'};
  char_9 = 'R';
  char char_11{'L'};
  char_1 = 'O';
  char char_13{'t'};
  print("{}{}{}",
        char_9, char_1, char_11);
}

// Answer (3):

// __ __ __
```

Puzzle 6

```
void run() {
  char char_1{'y'};
  char_1 = 'n';
  char char_3{'v'};
  char_3 = 'b';
  char char_5{'e'};
  char_1 = 'x';
  char char_7{'d'};
  char_5 = 'b';
  char char_9{'t'};
  char_3 = 'e';
  char char_11{'h'};
  char_5 = 'm';
  char char_13{'b'};
  print("{}{}",
        char_9, char_5);
}
```

```
// Answer (2):

// __ __
```

Puzzle 7

```
void run() {
  char char_1{'g'};
  char char_2{'o'};
  char_1 = 'r';
  char char_4{'q'};
  char_4 = 'n';
  char char_6{'q'};
  char_2 = 'f';
  char char_8{'x'};
  char_1 = 'r';
  char char_10{'e'};
  char_4 = 'n';
  char char_12{'g'};
  char_12 = 'u';
  char char_14{'w'};
  print("{}{}{}",
        char_10, char_1, char_2);
}

// Answer (3):

// __ __ __
```

Puzzle 8

```
void run() {
  char char_1{'j'};
  char_1 = 'c';
  char char_3{'m'};
  char_1 = 'g';
  char char_5{'g'};
  char_3 = 'd';
  char char_7{'w'};
  char_5 = 's';
  char char_9{'a'};
  char_7 = 't';
```

```
    char char_11{'b'};
    char_7 = 'e';
    char char_13{'c'};
    char_1 = 'c';
    char char_15{'b'};
    print("{}{}{}{}",
          char_3, char_7, char_1, char_9);
}

// Answer (4):

// __ __ __ __
```

Copies

Copy Example 1

```cpp
void run()
{
  int value = 4;
  auto copy = value;
  print("{}", copy);
}

// Answer: 4
```

Copy Example 2

```cpp
void run()
{
  int value = 4;
  auto copy = value;
  copy = 7;
  print("{}", copy);
}

// Answer: 7
```

Copy Example 3

```cpp
void run()
{
  int value = 4;
  auto copy = value;
  copy = 7;
  print("{}", value);
}

// Answer: 4
```

char **Copy Puzzles**

Puzzle 9

```
void run() {
  char char_1{'s'};
  auto char_2 = char_1;
  char_2 = 'm';
  char char_4{'w'};
  char_2 = 'p';
  char char_6{'g'};
  auto char_7 = char_1;
  print("{}{}",
        char_4, char_7);
}

// Answer (2):

// __ __
```

Puzzle 10

```
void run() {
  char char_1{'f'};
  auto char_2 = char_1;
  char char_3{'d'};
  auto char_4 = char_1;
  char char_5{'i'};
  print("{}{}",
        char_5, char_4);
}

// Answer (2):

// __ __
```

Puzzle 11

```
void run() {
  char char_1{'e'};
  char_1 = 'y';
  char char_3{'r'};
  auto char_4 = char_3;
  char_3 = 'e';
  auto char_6 = char_3;
  char char_7{'a'};
  char_1 = 'f';
  char char_9{'t'};
  print("{}{}{}{}",
        char_9, char_6, char_4, char_7);
}

// Answer (4):

// __ __ __ __
```

Puzzle 12

```
void run() {
  char char_1{'v'};
  auto char_2 = char_1;
  char_1 = 'h';
  auto char_4 = char_2;
  char_2 = 'u';
  auto char_6 = char_4;
  char_2 = 'R';
  char char_8{'O'};
  auto char_9 = char_2;
  print("{}{}{}",
        char_2, char_8, char_9);
}

// Answer (3):

// __ __ __
```

Puzzle 13

```
void run() {
  char char_1{'d'};
  auto char_2 = char_1;
  char_2 = 'q';
  char char_4{'e'};
  char_2 = 'n';
  char char_6{'a'};
  auto char_7 = char_6;
  char char_8{'m'};
  char_1 = 'x';
  auto char_10 = char_7;
  print("{}{}{}",
        char_4, char_1, char_7);
}

// Answer (3):

// __ __ __
```

Puzzle 14

```
void run() {
  char char_1{'d'};
  char char_2{'n'};
  char_1 = 'b';
  auto char_4 = char_2;
  char_1 = 'd';
  auto char_6 = char_1;
  char char_7{'f'};
  auto char_8 = char_6;
  char_7 = 'a';
  auto char_10 = char_2;
  print("{}{}{}",
        char_2, char_7, char_10);
}

// Answer (3):

// __ __ __
```

Puzzle 15

```cpp
void run() {
  char char_1{'v'};
  auto char_2 = char_1;
  char char_3{'p'};
  auto char_4 = char_3;
  char char_5{'v'};
  char_4 = 'w';
  char char_7{'k'};
  char_1 = 'o';
  char char_9{'w'};
  char_4 = 'f';
  auto char_11 = char_9;
  print("{}{}{}",
        char_3, char_1, char_9);
}

// Answer (3):

// __ __ __
```

Puzzle 16

```cpp
void run() {
  char char_1{'r'};
  char_1 = 'm';
  char char_3{'i'};
  auto char_4 = char_1;
  char_4 = 'M';
  char char_6{'v'};
  char_1 = 'u';
  auto char_8 = char_3;
  char_3 = 'e';
  auto char_10 = char_3;
  char char_11{'o'};
  auto char_12 = char_11;
  print("{}{}{}{}",
        char_4, char_11, char_6, char_3);
}

// Answer (4):

// __ __ __ __
```

References

Reference Example 1

```cpp
void run()
{
  int value = 4;
  auto &reference = value;
  print("{}", reference);
}

// Answer: 4
```

Reference Example 2

```cpp
void run()
{
  int value = 4;
  auto &reference = value;
  reference = 11;
  print("{}", reference);
}

// Answer: 11
```

Reference Example 3

```cpp
void run()
{
  int value = 4;
  auto &reference = value;
  reference = 11;
  print("{}", value);
}

// Answer: 11
```

char Reference Puzzles

Puzzle 17

```cpp
void run() {
  char char_1{'i'};
  auto &char_2 = char_1;
  char_2 = 'g';
  auto &char_4 = char_1;
  char_4 = 'd';
  char char_6{'o'};
  auto &char_7 = char_6;
  print("{}{}",
        char_1, char_7);
}

// Answer (2):

// __ __
```

Puzzle 18

```cpp
void run() {
  char char_1{'e'};
  char_1 = 'v';
  char char_3{'c'};
  char_1 = 'm';
  char char_5{'p'};
  auto &char_6 = char_5;
  char_5 = 'n';
  char char_8{'i'};
  print("{}{}{}",
        char_1, char_8, char_6);
}

// Answer (3):

// __ __ __
```

Puzzle 19

```
void run() {
  char char_1{'s'};
  auto &char_2 = char_1;
  char_1 = 'd';
  auto &char_4 = char_1;
  char char_5{'k'};
  char_5 = 'C';
  char char_7{'q'};
  char_2 = 'R';
  auto &char_9 = char_1;
  print("{}{}{}",
        char_1, char_5, char_4);
}

// Answer (3):

// __ __ __
```

Puzzle 20

```
void run() {
  char char_1{'d'};
  auto &char_2 = char_1;
  char char_3{'n'};
  char_2 = 'c';
  char char_5{'F'};
  char_2 = 'q';
  auto &char_7 = char_1;
  char_1 = 'L';
  char char_9{'S'};
  print("{}{}{}",
        char_7, char_5, char_9);
}

// Answer (3):

// __ __ __
```

Puzzle 21

```cpp
void run() {
  char char_1{'i'};
  auto &char_2 = char_1;
  char_1 = 'p';
  auto &char_4 = char_2;
  char_1 = 'l';
  char char_6{'L'};
  auto &char_7 = char_2;
  char char_8{'y'};
  char_1 = 'S';
  auto &char_10 = char_4;
  print("{}{}{}",
        char_6, char_1, char_2);
}

// Answer (3):

// __ __ __
```

Puzzle 22

```cpp
void run() {
  char char_1{'s'};
  auto &char_2 = char_1;
  char_2 = 'w';
  char char_4{'i'};
  char_2 = 'S';
  char char_6{'g'};
  auto &char_7 = char_2;
  char_4 = 'C';
  char char_9{'A'};
  char_6 = 's';
  auto &char_11 = char_2;
  print("{}{}{}{}",
        char_7, char_4, char_9, char_1);
}

// Answer (4):

// __ __ __ __
```

Puzzle 23

```cpp
void run() {
  char char_1{'w'};
  auto &char_2 = char_1;
  char_2 = 'r';
  auto &char_4 = char_1;
  char char_5{'w'};
  char_4 = 'e';
  char char_7{'R'};
  auto &char_8 = char_1;
  char_5 = 'P';
  char char_10{'o'};
  char_2 = 'E';
  auto &char_12 = char_8;
  print("{}{}{}{}",
        char_7, char_1, char_5, char_2);
}

// Answer (4):

// __ __ __ __
```

Puzzle 24

```cpp
void run() {
  char char_1{'w'};
  auto &char_2 = char_1;
  char_2 = 'a';
  auto &char_4 = char_2;
  char char_5{'k'};
  auto &char_6 = char_4;
  char_6 = 'q';
  char char_8{'m'};
  char_4 = 'v';
  char char_10{'a'};
  char_2 = 's';
  char char_12{'m'};
  print("{}{}{}",
        char_10, char_1, char_8);
}

// Answer (3):
```

```
// __ __ __
```

Puzzle 25

```
void run() {
  char char_1{'a'};
  char_1 = 'r';
  print("{}",
        char_1);
  char char_3{'q'};
  auto char_4 = char_3;
  char char_5{'s'};
  char_3 = 'i';
  char char_7{'u'};
  auto char_8 = char_1;
  char char_9{'e'};
  auto &char_10 = char_7;
  print("{}{}{}",
        char_9, char_4, char_7);
  auto char_11 = char_1;
  char char_12{'e'};
  print("{}{}{}{}",
        char_3, char_11, char_12, char_5);
}

// Answer (8):

// __ __ __ __ __ __ __ __
```

Puzzle 26

```
void run() {
  char char_1{'u'};
  char_1 = 't';
  auto char_3 = char_1;
  char_1 = 'r';
  char char_5{'o'};
  auto char_6 = char_1;
  auto &char_7 = char_3;
  char char_8{'l'};
  char_1 = 's';
  print("{}{}{}",
```

```
      char_1, char_7, char_6);
  auto &char_10 = char_5;
  char char_11{'d'};
  char_5 = 'p';
  char char_13{'o'};
  auto char_14 = char_10;
  print("{}{}{}",
        char_3, char_13, char_11);
}

// Answer (6):

// __ __ __ __ __ __
```

Puzzle 27

```
void run() {
  char char_1{'S'};
  auto &char_2 = char_1;
  auto char_3 = char_1;
  char_2 = 'v';
  auto &char_5 = char_1;
  char_5 = 'D';
  auto char_7 = char_2;
  char_7 = 'r';
  auto &char_9 = char_3;
  char char_10{'w'};
  auto char_11 = char_1;
  char_11 = 'y';
  auto char_13 = char_7;
  char char_14{'L'};
  print("{}{}{}",
        char_14, char_1, char_3);
}

// Answer (3):

// __ __ __
```

Puzzle 28

```cpp
void run() {
  char char_1{'T'};
  auto char_2 = char_1;
  auto &char_3 = char_2;
  auto char_4 = char_1;
  char_3 = 'c';
  char char_6{'q'};
  char_3 = 'S';
  auto char_8 = char_3;
  char char_9{'x'};
  char_6 = 'k';
  auto char_11 = char_2;
  char char_12{'O'};
  auto char_13 = char_6;
  print("{}{}{}{}",
        char_11, char_1, char_12, char_3);
}

// Answer (4):

// __ __ __ __
```

Puzzle 29

```cpp
void run() {
  char char_1{'t'};
  char_1 = 's';
  print("{}",
        char_1);
  auto char_3 = char_1;
  char_1 = 'j';
  char char_5{'d'};
  auto char_6 = char_1;
  char_6 = 'q';
  auto &char_8 = char_1;
  auto char_9 = char_5;
  auto &char_10 = char_9;
  char char_11{'b'};
  auto &char_12 = char_10;
  char_1 = 'e';
  auto &char_14 = char_1;
```

```
  auto char_15 = char_12;
  print("{}{}{}",
        char_14, char_8, char_12);
}

// Answer (4):


// __ __ __ __
```

Puzzle 30

```
void run() {
  char char_1{'S'};
  auto &char_2 = char_1;
  char char_3{'F'};
  print("{}{}",
        char_3, char_2);
  char_2 = 'B';
  char char_5{'x'};
  char_5 = 'U';
  auto char_7 = char_1;
  char_3 = 'R';
  char char_9{'s'};
  auto char_10 = char_3;
  auto &char_11 = char_9;
  char_9 = 'P';
  auto &char_13 = char_9;
  char char_14{'l'};
  auto char_15 = char_10;
  print("{}{}{}{}",
        char_5, char_7, char_15, char_13);
}

// Answer (6):


// __ __ __ __ __ __
```

Puzzle 31

```
void run() {
  char char_1{'u'};
  char char_2{'b'};
  char_1 = 'i';
  char char_4{'n'};
  char_2 = 's';
  auto &char_6 = char_4;
  char_4 = 't';
  char char_8{'m'};
  char_8 = 'o';
  char char_10{'c'};
  auto char_11 = char_2;
  char_4 = 'r';
  auto char_13 = char_8;
  char_2 = 'j';
  char char_15{'_'};
  auto &char_16 = char_4;
  char_2 = 'm';
  char char_18{'e'};
  print("{}{}{}{}{}{}{}",
        char_1, char_13, char_15, char_18, char_16, char_6,
        char_10);
}


// Answer (7):

// __ __ __ __ __ __ __
```

Puzzle 32

```
void run() {
  char char_1{'o'};
  char char_2{'l'};
  auto char_3 = char_2;
  auto &char_4 = char_2;
  char_3 = 'd';
  auto &char_6 = char_1;
  auto char_7 = char_3;
  char char_8{'w'};
  char_8 = 'w';
  auto &char_10 = char_7;
```

```
  char_8 = 'p';
  auto &char_12 = char_2;
  char char_13{'A'};
  auto char_14 = char_8;
  print("{}{}{}",
        char_13, char_3, char_7);
}

// Answer (3):

// __ __ __
```

Puzzle 33

```
void run() {
  char char_1{'q'};
  char_1 = '.';
  auto char_3 = char_1;
  char_1 = 'c';
  print("{}",
        char_1);
  auto &char_5 = char_3;
  auto char_6 = char_1;
  char_6 = 'f';
  auto char_8 = char_1;
  auto &char_9 = char_5;
  char_6 = 'p';
  char char_11{'p'};
  auto &char_12 = char_6;
  char char_13{'l'};
  char_1 = 'w';
  char char_15{'s'};
  print("{}{}{}{}",
        char_12, char_6, char_9, char_15);
  char_3 = 'e';
  char char_17{'o'};
  print("{}{}{}{}",
        char_8, char_17, char_11, char_3);
}

// Answer (9):

// __ __ __ __ __ __ __ __ __
```

Puzzle 34

```cpp
void run() {
  char char_1{'P'};
  auto &char_2 = char_1;
  print("{}",
        char_1);
  auto char_3 = char_2;
  char char_4{'H'};
  print("{}",
        char_4);
  char_1 = 'D';
  auto &char_6 = char_1;
  auto char_7 = char_2;
  char_7 = 'd';
  char char_9{'u'};
  auto char_10 = char_1;
  char char_11{'f'};
  char_3 = 'A';
  char char_13{'b'};
  auto char_14 = char_2;
  print("{}{}{}{}",
        char_3, char_6, char_2, char_14);
}

// Answer (6):

// __ __ __ __ __ __
```

Puzzle 35

```cpp
void run() {
  char char_1{'k'};
  char_1 = 'e';
  auto &char_3 = char_1;
  char char_4{'n'};
  char_3 = 'a';
  auto &char_6 = char_4;
  char char_7{'t'};
  char_7 = 'a';
  char char_9{'g'};
  auto char_10 = char_7;
  char char_11{'o'};
```

```
  char_9 = 'q';
  auto char_13 = char_3;
  char_10 = 'o';
  auto char_15 = char_3;
  char char_16{'a'};
  print("{}{}{}{}",
        char_4, char_3, char_6, char_11);
}

// Answer (4):

// __ __ __ __
```

Puzzle 36

```
void run() {
  char char_1{'d'};
  auto char_2 = char_1;
  char_2 = 'w';
  auto char_4 = char_1;
  auto &char_5 = char_1;
  char_2 = 'e';
  auto &char_7 = char_4;
  char_4 = 'n';
  char char_9{'h'};
  auto char_10 = char_1;
  char_10 = 'e';
  auto char_12 = char_4;
  auto &char_13 = char_5;
  char_12 = 'p';
  auto &char_15 = char_13;
  auto char_16 = char_1;
  print("{}{}{}",
        char_10, char_4, char_5);
}

// Answer (3):

// __ __ __
```

Puzzle 37

```
void run() {
  char char_1{'f'};
  char_1 = 'r';
  char char_3{'c'};
  char_3 = 'w';
  auto &char_5 = char_3;
  auto char_6 = char_5;
  print("{}",
        char_6);
  char_3 = 'h';
  auto &char_8 = char_6;
  char char_9{'c'};
  char_6 = 'o';
  char char_11{'m'};
  auto &char_12 = char_11;
  char char_13{'b'};
  char_3 = 'f';
  auto &char_15 = char_12;
  auto char_16 = char_3;
  char_6 = 't';
  char char_18{'o'};
  print("{}{}{}{}{}{}",
        char_9, char_1, char_8, char_18, char_11, char_13);
}

// Answer (7):

// __ __ __ __ __ __ __
```

Puzzle 38

```
void run() {
  char char_1{'r'};
  char_1 = 't';
  print("{}",
        char_1);
  auto char_3 = char_1;
  char_1 = 'm';
  auto char_5 = char_3;
  char char_6{'f'};
  auto char_7 = char_6;
```

```cpp
  char_6 = 'g';
  char char_9{'a'};
  auto &char_10 = char_3;
  char char_11{'q'};
  char_5 = 'k';
  char char_13{'m'};
  auto &char_14 = char_6;
  char char_15{'a'};
  auto char_16 = char_1;
  print("{}{}{}{}{}{}",
        char_14, char_15, char_16, char_13, char_9, char_7);
}

// Answer (7):

// __ __ __ __ __ __ __
```

Puzzle 39

```cpp
void run() {
  char char_1{'j'};
  char_1 = 'm';
  auto char_3 = char_1;
  print("{}",
        char_3);
  char_3 = 'g';
  char char_5{'r'};
  auto &char_6 = char_3;
  char_6 = 'e';
  char char_8{'w'};
  char_5 = 'q';
  auto char_10 = char_1;
  char char_11{'o'};
  char_10 = 'd';
  char char_13{'k'};
  auto &char_14 = char_10;
  auto char_15 = char_3;
  char_5 = 'v';
  char char_17{'m'};
  auto &char_18 = char_6;
  print("{}{}{}{}{}{}",
        char_15, char_17, char_1, char_11, char_5, char_6);
}
```

```
// Answer (7):

// __ __ __ __ __ __ __
```

Puzzle 40

```
void run() {
  char char_1{'b'};
  char_1 = 'm';
  auto &char_3 = char_1;
  char char_4{'t'};
  char_1 = 'h';
  auto char_6 = char_4;
  char char_7{'g'};
  char_1 = 'o';
  auto &char_9 = char_4;
  char char_10{'n'};
  auto &char_11 = char_7;
  char char_12{'b'};
  auto char_13 = char_11;
  char char_14{'i'};
  char_9 = 'l';
  char char_16{'l'};
  print("{}{}{}{}{}{}",
        char_14, char_9, char_1, char_13, char_12, char_16);
}
```

```
// Answer (6):

// __ __ __ __ __ __
```

Puzzle 41

```
void run() {
  char char_1{'L'};
  auto char_2 = char_1;
  char char_3{'o'};
  auto char_4 = char_1;
  char char_5{'b'};
  char_1 = 'D';
  char char_7{'2'};
  char_5 = 'E';
```

```cpp
  auto char_9 = char_1;
  char char_10{'s'};
  char_9 = 'x';
  auto &char_12 = char_7;
  auto char_13 = char_9;
  auto &char_14 = char_4;
  char char_15{'F'};
  print("{}{}{}{}{}{}",
        char_15, char_14, char_1, char_4, char_12, char_5);
}
```

```cpp
// Answer (6):


// __ __ __ __ __ __
```

Puzzle 42

```cpp
void run() {
  char char_1{'r'};
  auto char_2 = char_1;
  auto &char_3 = char_1;
  auto char_4 = char_1;
  char char_5{'s'};
  char_4 = 'r';
  auto char_7 = char_2;
  char_2 = 'm';
  auto char_9 = char_7;
  char_2 = 'o';
  char char_11{'r'};
  char_9 = 'd';
  auto char_13 = char_5;
  char char_14{'t'};
  auto &char_15 = char_5;
  char char_16{'e'};
  print("{}{}{}{}{}{}{}{}",
        char_13, char_14, char_4, char_16, char_3, char_1,
        char_2, char_11);
}
```

```cpp
// Answer (8):


// __ __ __ __ __ __ __ __
```

Puzzle 43

```cpp
void run() {
  char char_1{'n'};
  auto char_2 = char_1;
  char char_3{'s'};
  char_2 = 's';
  print("{}",
        char_2);
  char char_5{'p'};
  auto &char_6 = char_1;
  char_6 = ':';
  print("{}",
        char_5);
  char char_8{'i'};
  char_2 = 'n';
  auto &char_10 = char_2;
  char char_11{'a'};
  print("{}{}{}{}",
        char_11, char_10, char_6, char_1);
  auto &char_12 = char_3;
  print("{}",
        char_3);
  char_12 = 'z';
  print("{}",
        char_8);
  char char_14{'e'};
  print("{}",
        char_12);
  char char_15{'x'};
  auto &char_16 = char_12;
  print("{}",
        char_14);
}

// Answer (10):

// __ __ __ __ __ __ __ __ __ __
```

Puzzle 44

```
void run() {
  char char_1{'o'};
  char_1 = 'l';
  auto &char_3 = char_1;
  char char_4{'d'};
  auto char_5 = char_4;
  char_1 = 'k';
  char char_7{'g'};
  char_5 = 'n';
  print("{}",
        char_5);
  char char_9{'p'};
  auto &char_10 = char_3;
  auto char_11 = char_10;
  auto &char_12 = char_5;
  char char_13{'k'};
  auto char_14 = char_7;
  char_3 = 'o';
  auto char_16 = char_12;
  print("{}{}{}",
        char_1, char_10, char_9);
}

// Answer (4):

// __ __ __ __
```

Puzzle 45

```
void run() {
  char char_1{'w'};
  char_1 = 'o';
  char char_3{'i'};
  auto &char_4 = char_1;
  char char_5{'e'};
  auto char_6 = char_3;
  char_5 = 'y';
  char char_8{'a'};
  char_1 = 'p';
  auto char_10 = char_4;
  char_6 = 'o';
```

```
  auto &char_12 = char_8;
  char_8 = 'e';
  char char_14{'r'};
  auto &char_15 = char_6;
  char char_16{'k'};
  auto char_17 = char_6;
  char_15 = 'l';
  char char_19{'t'};
  print("{}{}{}{}",
        char_15, char_8, char_14, char_4);
}
```

```
// Answer (4):
```

```
// __ __ __ __
```

___

Puzzle 46

___

```
void run() {
  char char_1{'u'};
  char_1 = 'l';
  auto &char_3 = char_1;
  print("{}",
        char_3);
  char_1 = 'j';
  char char_5{'x'};
  auto &char_6 = char_1;
  char char_7{'j'};
  auto &char_8 = char_5;
  char char_9{'v'};
  auto &char_10 = char_6;
  char_10 = 'd';
  auto char_12 = char_5;
  char_5 = '_';
  auto char_14 = char_3;
  char char_15{'i'};
  auto char_16 = char_14;
  char char_17{'t'};
  print("{}{}{}{}{}",
        char_16, char_15, char_9, char_8, char_17);
}
```

```
// Answer (6):
```

```
// __ __ __ __ __ __
```

Puzzle 47

```cpp
void run() {
  char char_1{'q'};
  char char_2{'c'};
  char_1 = '.';
  char char_4{'n'};
  print("{}",
        char_2);
  char_2 = 'y';
  auto char_6 = char_1;
  char_6 = 'p';
  auto char_8 = char_4;
  auto &char_9 = char_2;
  char_8 = 'x';
  auto char_11 = char_2;
  char_11 = 'q';
  char char_13{'n'};
  auto &char_14 = char_9;
  char char_15{'p'};
  char_13 = 'u';
  auto char_17 = char_13;
  char char_18{'a'};
  print("{}{}{}{}{}",
        char_15, char_6, char_1, char_4, char_17);
  char_2 = 'l';
  char char_20{'c'};
  print("{}{}",
        char_14, char_9);
}

// Answer (8):

// __ __ __ __ __ __ __ __
```

Puzzle 48

```cpp
void run() {
  char char_1{'i'};
  auto &char_2 = char_1;
  char_2 = 'g';
  print("{}",
        char_2);
  char_1 = 'e';
  print("{}",
        char_1);
  char_2 = 'n';
  auto char_6 = char_2;
  char char_7{'a'};
  print("{}",
        char_6);
  char_2 = 'e';
  auto char_9 = char_2;
  auto &char_10 = char_7;
  auto char_11 = char_9;
  char_1 = 'i';
  auto &char_13 = char_6;
  char_1 = 'y';
  auto &char_15 = char_13;
  char char_16{'t'};
  auto char_17 = char_2;
  char_2 = 'u';
  char char_19{'r'};
  auto char_20 = char_11;
  print("{}{}{}{}{}",
        char_20, char_19, char_7, char_16, char_11);
}

// Answer (8):

// _ _ _ _ _ _ _ _
```

Puzzle 49

```cpp
void run() {
  char char_1{'v'};
  char_1 = 'r';
  auto char_3 = char_1;
  auto &char_4 = char_1;
  auto char_5 = char_3;
  char char_6{'p'};
  auto &char_7 = char_3;
  char char_8{'g'};
  auto char_9 = char_3;
  auto &char_10 = char_6;
  char_10 = 't';
  auto &char_12 = char_8;
  char_3 = 's';
  auto char_14 = char_10;
  char_1 = 'k';
  auto char_16 = char_9;
  char char_17{'s'};
  print("{}{}{}{}{}{}",
        char_17, char_14, char_9, char_7, char_6, char_16);
}


// Answer (6):


// __ __ __ __ __ __
```

Puzzle 50

```cpp
void run() {
  char char_1{'l'};
  auto &char_2 = char_1;
  char char_3{'v'};
  auto &char_4 = char_1;
  auto char_5 = char_2;
  print("{}{}",
        char_4, char_5);
  auto &char_6 = char_3;
  auto char_7 = char_1;
  auto &char_8 = char_3;
  char char_9{'q'};
  char_3 = 's';
```

```cpp
  auto &char_11 = char_9;
  char_11 = 'a';
  auto char_13 = char_2;
  char_5 = 'g';
  char char_15{'b'};
  auto char_16 = char_9;
  print("{}{}{}",
        char_16, char_15, char_3);
}

// Answer (5):


// __ __ __ __ __
```

Puzzle 51

```cpp
void run() {
  char char_1{'n'};
  char_1 = 'i';
  char char_3{'t'};
  auto char_4 = char_3;
  auto &char_5 = char_1;
  auto char_6 = char_1;
  char_1 = 'n';
  print("{}{}",
        char_6, char_1);
  char char_8{'t'};
  char_1 = '8';
  auto &char_10 = char_6;
  char_6 = 'd';
  auto char_12 = char_5;
  char char_13{'q'};
  auto &char_14 = char_8;
  char char_15{'c'};
  auto char_16 = char_3;
  char_8 = '_';
  auto char_18 = char_10;
  print("{}{}{}{}",
        char_4, char_5, char_14, char_16);
}

// Answer (6):
```

```
// __ __ __ __ __ __
```

Puzzle 52

```cpp
void run() {
  char char_1{'a'};
  char_1 = 'r';
  auto char_3 = char_1;
  char_3 = 'p';
  char char_5{'t'};
  auto char_6 = char_3;
  auto &char_7 = char_3;
  char_1 = 'm';
  auto char_9 = char_1;
  char char_10{'y'};
  auto &char_11 = char_3;
  char_10 = 'y';
  char char_13{'d'};
  char_7 = 'a';
  auto char_15 = char_9;
  auto &char_16 = char_3;
  char char_17{'g'};
  auto char_18 = char_17;
  print("{}{}{}{}{}{}",
        char_5, char_18, char_3, char_15, char_9, char_11);
}
```

```
// Answer (6):
```

```
// __ __ __ __ __ __
```

Puzzle 53

```cpp
void run() {
  char char_1{'q'};
  auto char_2 = char_1;
  char char_3{'y'};
  char_2 = 'm';
  char char_5{'o'};
  auto &char_6 = char_1;
  char_3 = '_';
  char char_8{'g'};
```

```cpp
  auto char_9 = char_2;
  char_1 = 'x';
  char char_11{'f'};
  auto &char_12 = char_8;
  char char_13{'a'};
  auto char_14 = char_8;
  char_14 = 'l';
  char char_16{'v'};
  auto &char_17 = char_9;
  char_1 = 'l';
  auto &char_19 = char_12;
  print("{}{}{}{}{}{}",
        char_13, char_6, char_1, char_3, char_5, char_11);
}

// Answer (6):

// __ __ __ __ __ __
```

Puzzle 54

```cpp
void run() {
  char char_1{'s'};
  auto char_2 = char_1;
  char char_3{'h'};
  auto char_4 = char_1;
  char char_5{'d'};
  char_3 = 'e';
  char char_7{'a'};
  auto &char_8 = char_3;
  char char_9{'g'};
  char_1 = 's';
  auto &char_11 = char_1;
  auto char_12 = char_4;
  char char_13{'b'};
  auto char_14 = char_13;
  char char_15{'m'};
  auto &char_16 = char_7;
  print("{}{}{}{}{}{}{}{}",
        char_15, char_3, char_12, char_1, char_7, char_9,
        char_8, char_11);
}
```

```
// Answer (8):

// __ __ __ __ __ __ __ __
```

Puzzle 55

```
void run() {
  char char_1{'x'};
  auto &char_2 = char_1;
  char_1 = 'u';
  auto &char_4 = char_1;
  char_2 = 'g';
  print("{}",
        char_4);
  char_1 = 'r';
  print("{}",
        char_2);
  char_2 = 'l';
  auto char_8 = char_1;
  char char_9{'a'};
  auto &char_10 = char_2;
  char char_11{'u'};
  char_11 = '.';
  char char_13{'m'};
  auto &char_14 = char_10;
  char_10 = 'g';
  char char_16{'p'};
  char_1 = 'c';
  auto char_18 = char_4;
  char char_19{'d'};
  auto char_20 = char_14;
  auto &char_21 = char_11;
  print("{}{}{}{}{}{}",
        char_9, char_13, char_11, char_19, char_10, char_8);
}

// Answer (8):

// __ __ __ __ __ __ __ __
```

Puzzle 56

```cpp
void run() {
  char char_1{'e'};
  auto char_2 = char_1;
  char_1 = 'r';
  auto &char_4 = char_1;
  char char_5{'t'};
  print("{}{}",
        char_4, char_2);
  auto &char_6 = char_1;
  char char_7{'h'};
  char_5 = 'a';
  char char_9{'t'};
  auto &char_10 = char_6;
  char char_11{'e'};
  auto &char_12 = char_9;
  char char_13{'u'};
  char_12 = 'l';
  char char_15{'w'};
  auto char_16 = char_12;
  char_11 = 'g';
  auto char_18 = char_10;
  print("{}{}{}{}{}",
        char_11, char_13, char_12, char_5, char_10);
}

// Answer (7):

// __ __ __ __ __ __ __
```

Puzzle 57

```cpp
void run() {
  char char_1{'w'};
  auto &char_2 = char_1;
  char char_3{'d'};
  auto &char_4 = char_1;
  print("{}",
        char_2);
  auto &char_5 = char_3;
  char char_6{'b'};
  auto &char_7 = char_1;
```

```cpp
  char_6 = 't';
  char char_9{'d'};
  auto &char_10 = char_1;
  char_6 = 'w';
  auto &char_12 = char_1;
  char_4 = 'c';
  auto &char_14 = char_4;
  char_3 = 'p';
  char char_16{'w'};
  char_9 = 's';
  auto &char_18 = char_9;
  char char_19{'n'};
  print("{}{}{}{}{}{}",
        char_1, char_18, char_14, char_9, char_3, char_19);
}

// Answer (7):

// __ __ __ __ __ __ __
```

Puzzle 58

```cpp
void run() {
  char char_1{'k'};
  auto &char_2 = char_1;
  auto char_3 = char_1;
  char char_4{'P'};
  char_2 = 's';
  auto char_6 = char_4;
  auto &char_7 = char_4;
  char_2 = 'c';
  auto char_9 = char_3;
  char_4 = 'm';
  char char_11{'O'};
  auto &char_12 = char_1;
  char char_13{'L'};
  auto &char_14 = char_4;
  char char_15{'j'};
  char_7 = 'u';
  auto char_17 = char_6;
  char_15 = 'O';
  auto char_19 = char_14;
  print("{}{}{}{}{}{}",
```

```
        char_13, char_15, char_11, char_17, char_1, char_2);
}

// Answer (6):

// __ __ __ __ __ __
```

Puzzle 59

```
void run() {
  char char_1{'t'};
  char char_2{'e'};
  auto &char_3 = char_2;
  char char_4{'d'};
  auto &char_5 = char_4;
  auto char_6 = char_3;
  print("{}{}",
        char_4, char_3);
  auto char_7 = char_1;
  auto &char_8 = char_7;
  auto char_9 = char_6;
  char char_10{'l'};
  auto &char_11 = char_4;
  char_8 = 'e';
  auto &char_13 = char_8;
  auto char_14 = char_1;
  char char_15{'t'};
  print("{}{}{}{}",
        char_10, char_6, char_14, char_13);
}

// Answer (6):

// __ __ __ __ __ __
```

Puzzle 60

```
void run() {
  char char_1{'u'};
  auto &char_2 = char_1;
  char_2 = 'O';
  auto &char_4 = char_2;
  char char_5{'b'};
  auto &char_6 = char_5;
  char_5 = 'F';
  auto char_8 = char_6;
  char_5 = 'P';
  char char_10{'Q'};
  auto char_11 = char_4;
  auto &char_12 = char_8;
  auto char_13 = char_10;
  auto &char_14 = char_6;
  auto char_15 = char_6;
  auto &char_16 = char_10;
  auto char_17 = char_1;
  print("{}{}{}{}{}",
        char_6, char_2, char_5, char_12, char_13);
}

// Answer (5):

// __ __ __ __ __
```

Puzzle 61

```
void run() {
  char char_1{'q'};
  auto char_2 = char_1;
  auto &char_3 = char_2;
  char char_4{'a'};
  char_3 = 'r';
  auto char_6 = char_4;
  auto &char_7 = char_1;
  char char_8{'y'};
  auto &char_9 = char_3;
  auto char_10 = char_2;
  char_7 = 'p';
  char char_12{'g'};
```

```cpp
    auto &char_13 = char_9;
    auto char_14 = char_3;
    char_7 = 'n';
    auto char_16 = char_8;
    char char_17{'a'};
    auto &char_18 = char_2;
    print("{}{}{}{}{}",
          char_17, char_9, char_13, char_4, char_16);
}

// Answer (5):

// __ __ __ __ __
```

Puzzle 62

```cpp
void run() {
  char char_1{'r'};
  print("{}",
        char_1);
  char char_2{'f'};
  auto char_3 = char_2;
  char char_4{'.'};
  char_2 = 'e';
  print("{}{}",
        char_2, char_4);
  char char_6{'n'};
  auto &char_7 = char_2;
  auto char_8 = char_1;
  char_1 = 'c';
  auto char_10 = char_2;
  char_3 = 'r';
  char char_12{'x'};
  char_8 = 'i';
  char char_14{'x'};
  auto &char_15 = char_1;
  char_10 = 'r';
  char char_17{'e'};
  auto char_18 = char_1;
  char_8 = 'f';
  auto &char_20 = char_6;
  char_20 = 'g';
  auto &char_22 = char_20;
```

```
  print("{}{}{}{}{}",
        char_10, char_7, char_6, char_17, char_14);
}

// Answer (8):

// __ __ __ __ __ __ __ __
```

Puzzle 63

```
void run() {
  char char_1{'s'};
  auto char_2 = char_1;
  print("{}",
        char_1);
  auto char_3 = char_2;
  auto &char_4 = char_2;
  char_2 = 'l';
  char char_6{'f'};
  auto char_7 = char_6;
  char char_8{'n'};
  char_8 = 't';
  char char_10{'v'};
  auto &char_11 = char_3;
  auto char_12 = char_3;
  char_10 = '_';
  auto &char_14 = char_10;
  char char_15{'l'};
  char_7 = 'z';
  char char_17{'m'};
  char_17 = 'i';
  auto char_19 = char_3;
  char char_20{'e'};
  print("{}{}{}{}{}",
        char_17, char_7, char_20, char_14, char_8);
}

// Answer (6):

// __ __ __ __ __ __
```

Puzzle 64

```cpp
void run() {
  char char_1{'y'};
  char_1 = 'r';
  char char_3{'f'};
  char_3 = 'c';
  char char_5{'v'};
  auto &char_6 = char_3;
  char_6 = 'e';
  auto &char_8 = char_3;
  char char_9{'s'};
  auto char_10 = char_9;
  char char_11{'v'};
  auto char_12 = char_8;
  char char_13{'h'};
  char_5 = 'k';
  auto char_15 = char_13;
  char_5 = 'j';
  auto &char_17 = char_13;
  char_13 = 'r';
  auto char_19 = char_1;
  char_19 = 'r';
  char char_21{'e'};
  char_5 = 'y';
  auto &char_23 = char_11;
  print("{}{}{}{}{}{}{}",
        char_17, char_21, char_23, char_6, char_1, char_9,
        char_3);
}

// Answer (7):

// __ __ __ __ __ __ __
```

Functions

Function Example 1

```cpp
void update_copy(int parameter) {
  parameter = 5;
}

void run()
{
  int value = 7;
  update_copy(value);
  fmt::print("{}", value);
}

// Answer: 7
```

Function Example 2

```cpp
void update_reference(int &parameter) {
  parameter = 5;
}

void run()
{
  int value = 7;
  update_reference(value);
  fmt::print("{}", value);
}

// Answer: 5
```

char Puzzles With Functions

Puzzle 65

```
auto function(char &parameter_1, char parameter_2) {
  parameter_1 = 't';
  char char_2{':'};
  parameter_1 = 'd';
  auto char_4 = char_2;
  print("{}{}",
        parameter_1, parameter_2);
  char char_5{'i'};
  print("{}{}",
        char_2, char_5);
}
void run() {
  char char_1{'t'};
  auto char_2 = char_1;
  char_1 = 'd';
  print("{}",
        char_2);
  char char_4{'a'};
  char_1 = 'i';
  auto char_6 = char_2;
  char char_7{'r'};
  auto char_8 = char_6;
  char_8 = ':';
  auto char_10 = char_4;
  char_1 = 'w';
  char char_12{'h'};
  char_1 = 'e';
  char char_14{'d'};
  auto &char_15 = char_14;
  print("{}{}{}{}",
        char_12, char_7, char_1, char_10);
  function(char_10, char_8);
  print("{}",
        char_14);
}

// Answer (10):
```

```
// __ __ __ __ __ __ __ __ __ __
```

Puzzle 66

```
auto function(char &parameter_1, char &parameter_2) {
  char char_1{'a'};
  auto char_2 = char_1;
  print("{}",
        parameter_1);
  auto char_3 = parameter_1;
  char char_4{'g'};
  print("{}{}",
        char_4, char_1);
}
void run() {
  char char_1{'a'};
  char char_2{'m'};
  auto char_3 = char_2;
  auto &char_4 = char_2;
  char char_5{'l'};
  auto &char_6 = char_2;
  char char_7{'l'};
  auto char_8 = char_7;
  function(char_5, char_6);
  auto &char_9 = char_4;
  auto char_10 = char_1;
  print("{}{}{}{}",
        char_9, char_3, char_10, char_8);
}

// Answer (7):

// __ __ __ __ __ __ __ __
```

Puzzle 67

```cpp
auto function(char &parameter_1, char parameter_2) {
  parameter_2 = 'f';
  char char_2{'i'};
  auto &char_3 = parameter_1;
  char char_4{'l'};
  auto char_5 = parameter_1;
  parameter_2 = 'x';
  print("{}{}{}",
        char_2, char_3, parameter_1);
}
void run() {
  char char_1{'f'};
  auto char_2 = char_1;
  char char_3{'d'};
  auto char_4 = char_3;
  print("{}",
        char_4);
  char char_5{'v'};
  auto &char_6 = char_2;
  auto char_7 = char_3;
  function(char_6, char_3);
  char_2 = '.';
  auto char_9 = char_5;
  char_5 = 'p';
  char char_11{'c'};
  char_1 = 'p';
  char char_13{'r'};
  char_13 = 'b';
  auto &char_15 = char_7;
  print("{}{}{}{}",
        char_2, char_11, char_5, char_1);
}

// Answer (8):

// __ __ __ __ __ __ __ __
```

Puzzle 68

```
auto function(char &parameter_1, char parameter_2) {
  parameter_1 = 'b';
  char char_2{'p'};
  parameter_1 = 'i';
  auto char_4 = parameter_1;
  auto &char_5 = parameter_2;
  char char_6{'o'};
  print("{}{}{}",
        char_2, char_6, char_4);
}
void run() {
  char char_1{'q'};
  char char_2{'p'};
  char_1 = 'i';
  auto &char_4 = char_2;
  char char_5{'s'};
  char_5 = 'o';
  function(char_2, char_1);
  auto &char_7 = char_5;
  char char_8{'s'};
  auto &char_9 = char_5;
  auto char_10 = char_8;
  char char_11{'n'};
  auto &char_12 = char_4;
  auto char_13 = char_11;
  print("{}{}{}{}",
        char_10, char_8, char_5, char_13);
}

// Answer (7):

// __ __ __ __ __ __ __
```

Puzzle 69

```cpp
auto function(char &parameter_1, char parameter_2) {
  parameter_1 = 'w';
  char char_2{'e'};
  parameter_1 = 'b';
  auto &char_4 = parameter_1;
  parameter_2 = 'm';
  auto &char_6 = parameter_2;
  print("{}{}",
        char_6, char_2);
}
void run() {
  char char_1{'s'};
  auto &char_2 = char_1;
  auto char_3 = char_2;
  char char_4{'v'};
  char_2 = 'm';
  auto char_6 = char_4;
  char char_7{'r'};
  char_3 = 'g';
  char char_9{'o'};
  auto &char_10 = char_3;
  char_6 = 'f';
  char char_12{'c'};
  auto &char_13 = char_10;
  function(char_4, char_2);
  char char_14{'h'};
  print("{}{}{}{}",
        char_1, char_12, char_14, char_7);
}

// Answer (6):

// __ __ __ __ __ __
```

Puzzle 70

```cpp
auto function(char &parameter_1, char &parameter_2) {
  char char_1{'h'};
  auto char_2 = parameter_2;
  char char_3{'u'};
  auto &char_4 = char_1;
  char_1 = 'a';
  auto &char_6 = char_1;
  print("{}{}",
        char_1, char_2);
}
void run() {
  char char_1{'h'};
  auto char_2 = char_1;
  auto &char_3 = char_2;
  auto char_4 = char_1;
  char_3 = 'a';
  char char_6{'s'};
  print("{}",
        char_6);
  char_4 = 'y';
  char char_8{'s'};
  auto char_9 = char_8;
  char_3 = 'e';
  auto &char_11 = char_9;
  print("{}{}{}",
        char_4, char_8, char_2);
  char_9 = 'r';
  char char_13{'.'};
  auto char_14 = char_3;
  char char_15{'h'};
  print("{}{}{}{}",
        char_9, char_11, char_13, char_15);
  function(char_1, char_6);
  print("{}",
        char_1);
}

// Answer (11):

// __ __ __ __ __ __ __ __ __ __ __
```

Puzzle 71

```cpp
auto function(char &parameter_1, char parameter_2) {
  print("{}",
        parameter_1);
  parameter_2 = 'o';
  print("{}",
        parameter_2);
  parameter_2 = 'k';
  char char_3{'l'};
  auto char_4 = parameter_1;
  print("{}",
        char_4);
}
void run() {
  char char_1{'o'};
  auto char_2 = char_1;
  char char_3{'f'};
  auto &char_4 = char_3;
  char_2 = 'n';
  char char_6{'c'};
  char_4 = 'p';
  char char_8{'o'};
  auto char_9 = char_3;
  char char_10{'u'};
  function(char_3, char_10);
  char char_11{'y'};
  auto &char_12 = char_4;
  char_4 = 't';
  auto &char_14 = char_6;
  char_9 = 'a';
  auto char_16 = char_10;
  print("{}{}{}{}{}",
        char_14, char_8, char_10, char_2, char_12);
}

// Answer (8):

// __ __ __ __ __ __ __ __
```

Puzzle 72

```
auto function(char &parameter_1, char &parameter_2) {
  parameter_1 = 'Q';
  parameter_2 = 'g';
  char char_3{'o'};
  parameter_2 = 'V';
  char char_5{'V'};
  auto &char_6 = char_3;
  print("{}",
        parameter_2);
}
void run() {
  char char_1{'Q'};
  auto char_2 = char_1;
  auto &char_3 = char_2;
  char char_4{'V'};
  function(char_2, char_4);
  char char_5{'V'};
  char_3 = 'P';
  char char_7{'O'};
  auto &char_8 = char_4;
  char_4 = 'M';
  print("{}{}{}",
        char_3, char_8, char_7);
  char char_10{'s'};
  char_10 = 'f';
  auto char_12 = char_8;
  auto &char_13 = char_3;
  char_12 = '2';
  auto char_15 = char_12;
  char_13 = 'M';
  auto &char_17 = char_2;
  print("{}{}{}{}",
        char_5, char_1, char_12, char_2);
}

// Answer (8):

// __ __ __ __ __ __ __ __
```

Puzzle 73

```cpp
auto function(char &parameter_1, char parameter_2) {
  char char_1{'f'};
  auto &char_2 = char_1;
  char char_3{'m'};
  parameter_1 = 't';
  auto &char_5 = char_2;
  char_5 = 's';
  print("{}{}{}",
        char_1, parameter_1, char_3);
}
void run() {
  char char_1{'k'};
  char_1 = 'o';
  char char_3{'m'};
  char_1 = 't';
  auto char_5 = char_1;
  char char_6{'s'};
  auto &char_7 = char_5;
  auto char_8 = char_7;
  char_1 = '.';
  auto char_10 = char_1;
  auto &char_11 = char_7;
  char_10 = 't';
  function(char_11, char_6);
  auto char_13 = char_1;
  char char_14{'p'};
  auto &char_15 = char_11;
  char char_16{'t'};
  print("{}{}{}{}{}{}",
        char_16, char_13, char_6, char_11, char_3, char_5);
}


// Answer (9):

// __ __ __ __ __ __ __ __ __
```

Puzzle 74

```cpp
auto function(char &parameter_1, char parameter_2) {
  parameter_2 = 's';
  char char_2{'l'};
  auto char_3 = parameter_2;
  char char_4{'c'};
  auto &char_5 = char_4;
  char char_6{'a'};
  print("{}{}{}",
        char_6, char_3, parameter_2);
}
void run() {
  char char_1{'s'};
  char_1 = 'l';
  char char_3{'c'};
  char_3 = 'c';
  auto &char_5 = char_3;
  char char_6{'a'};
  print("{}{}",
        char_5, char_1);
  auto char_7 = char_1;
  auto &char_8 = char_1;
  char char_9{'.'};
  char_8 = 'b';
  char char_11{'t'};
  function(char_7, char_6);
  auto &char_12 = char_7;
  char char_13{'m'};
  char_8 = 'f';
  char char_15{'i'};
  auto &char_16 = char_1;
  print("{}{}{}{}{}",
        char_9, char_13, char_16, char_3, char_11);
}


// Answer (10):

// __ __ __ __ __ __ __ __ __ __
```

Puzzle 75

```
auto function(char parameter_1, char &parameter_2) {
  print("{}",
        parameter_2);
  char char_1{'o'};
  char_1 = 'h';
  auto &char_3 = parameter_1;
  parameter_1 = 'e';
  char char_5{'p'};
  print("{}{}",
        char_5, char_3);
}
void run() {
  char char_1{'o'};
  auto char_2 = char_1;
  char char_3{'x'};
  char_3 = 'e';
  char char_5{'p'};
  auto &char_6 = char_3;
  char_1 = 'r';
  function(char_1, char_2);
  char char_8{'n'};
  char_6 = 'e';
  auto char_10 = char_1;
  char char_11{'a'};
  char_3 = 'f';
  char char_13{'x'};
  char_1 = 't';
  char char_15{'h'};
  auto char_16 = char_10;
  auto &char_17 = char_6;
  auto char_18 = char_1;
  print("{}{}{}{}{}",
        char_10, char_11, char_1, char_2, char_16);
}

// Answer (8):

// __ __ __ __ __ __ __ __
```

Puzzle 76

```
auto function(char parameter_1, char &parameter_2) {
  parameter_2 = 'i';
  parameter_1 = 'j';
  char char_3{'s'};
  print("{}",
        parameter_2);
  parameter_1 = 'd';
  char char_5{'x'};
  print("{}{}",
        char_3, char_5);
}
void run() {
  char char_1{'i'};
  auto char_2 = char_1;
  function(char_1, char_2);
  auto &char_3 = char_1;
  char char_4{'d'};
  char_2 = 'x';
  char char_6{'t'};
  auto char_7 = char_2;
  char char_8{'g'};
  auto &char_9 = char_3;
  char_7 = 'i';
  auto &char_11 = char_8;
  char_9 = 'q';
  auto &char_13 = char_6;
  auto char_14 = char_1;
  char_3 = 'i';
  char char_16{'e'};
  auto &char_17 = char_4;
  print("{}{}{}{}{}",
        char_4, char_3, char_8, char_7, char_13);
}


// Answer (8):


// __ __ __ __ __ __ __ __
```

Puzzle 77

```cpp
auto function(char &parameter_1, char &parameter_2) {
  parameter_2 = 't';
  parameter_2 = 'f';
  char char_3{'s'};
  parameter_2 = 'a';
  char char_5{'y'};
  char_3 = 'x';
  print("{}",
        parameter_1);
}
void run() {
  char char_1{'b'};
  char_1 = 'c';
  auto &char_3 = char_1;
  char char_4{'a'};
  char_1 = 'd';
  function(char_1, char_3);
  auto &char_6 = char_1;
  auto char_7 = char_6;
  char char_8{'2'};
  auto &char_9 = char_7;
  char char_10{'n'};
  auto &char_11 = char_10;
  auto char_12 = char_10;
  char_3 = 'f';
  char char_14{'t'};
  auto char_15 = char_12;
  auto &char_16 = char_12;
  print("{}{}{}{}{}",
        char_14, char_4, char_16, char_8, char_1);
}

// Answer (6):

// __ __ __ __ __ __
```

Puzzle 78

```cpp
auto function(char &parameter_1, char parameter_2) {
  char char_1{'a'};
  char char_2{'f'};
  auto char_3 = parameter_2;
  char char_4{'p'};
  auto &char_5 = char_4;
  char_3 = 'o';
  print("{}{}{}",
        char_4, char_1, parameter_2);
}
void run() {
  char char_1{'a'};
  auto &char_2 = char_1;
  char_1 = 'd';
  auto char_4 = char_1;
  char_2 = 'n';
  char char_6{'o'};
  auto char_7 = char_1;
  char_1 = 'r';
  auto char_9 = char_4;
  auto &char_10 = char_2;
  char_4 = 't';
  function(char_9, char_2);
  char char_12{'i'};
  auto &char_13 = char_1;
  char char_14{'i'};
  auto &char_15 = char_12;
  char_14 = 'b';
  auto char_17 = char_9;
  char char_18{'t'};
  print("{}{}{}{}{}{}",
        char_18, char_15, char_4, char_12, char_6, char_7);
}

// Answer (9):

// __ __ __ __ __ __ __ __ __ __
```

Puzzle 79

```cpp
auto function(char &parameter_1, char &parameter_2) {
  char char_1{'r'};
  char_1 = 'r';
  auto &char_3 = parameter_2;
  parameter_1 = 'e';
  auto char_5 = parameter_2;
  char_3 = '.';
  print("{}{}{}",
        char_3, char_1, parameter_1);
}
void run() {
  char char_1{'r'};
  auto &char_2 = char_1;
  char char_3{'e'};
  print("{}{}",
        char_2, char_3);
  auto &char_4 = char_2;
  auto char_5 = char_2;
  char_1 = '.';
  auto &char_7 = char_5;
  function(char_5, char_4);
  auto char_8 = char_7;
  auto &char_9 = char_8;
  auto char_10 = char_9;
  auto &char_11 = char_9;
  char_4 = 'r';
  char char_13{'t'};
  auto &char_14 = char_10;
  char_14 = 'i';
  auto &char_16 = char_11;
  char char_17{'g'};
  print("{}{}{}{}{}",
        char_17, char_10, char_13, char_11, char_1);
}

// Answer (10):

// __ __ __ __ __ __ __ __ __ __
```

Puzzle 80

```cpp
auto function(char parameter_1, char &parameter_2) {
  parameter_1 = 'a';
  parameter_1 = 's';
  char char_3{'c'};
  auto char_4 = parameter_2;
  print("{}",
        parameter_1);
  auto &char_5 = char_3;
  print("{}",
        char_5);
}
void run() {
  char char_1{'a'};
  print("{}",
        char_1);
  char char_2{'s'};
  function(char_2, char_1);
  char_2 = 'c';
  auto char_4 = char_1;
  char_1 = 'v';
  auto &char_6 = char_4;
  char char_7{'t'};
  char_4 = 'i';
  char char_9{'e'};
  auto char_10 = char_4;
  auto &char_11 = char_6;
  char char_12{'y'};
  auto &char_13 = char_10;
  char char_14{'t'};
  char_2 = 'v';
  char char_16{'k'};
  char_2 = 'm';
  auto &char_18 = char_10;
  auto char_19 = char_11;
  print("{}{}{}{}",
        char_14, char_6, char_2, char_9);
}

// Answer (7):

// __ __ __ __ __ __ __
```

Puzzle 81

```
auto function(char &parameter_1, char parameter_2) {
  parameter_1 = 'e';
  print("{}",
        parameter_2);
  char char_2{'e'};
  auto &char_3 = char_2;
  char char_4{'y'};
  auto char_5 = char_4;
  print("{}",
        char_3);
}
void run() {
  char char_1{'u'};
  auto &char_2 = char_1;
  char_1 = 'g';
  char char_4{'g'};
  auto char_5 = char_1;
  char_4 = 'n';
  function(char_5, char_2);
  char char_7{'a'};
  char_1 = 'h';
  auto char_9 = char_7;
  char char_10{'e'};
  char_9 = 'a';
  char char_12{'c'};
  char_10 = 'o';
  auto char_14 = char_10;
  char_2 = 'r';
  auto char_16 = char_1;
  auto &char_17 = char_9;
  char_5 = 'e';
  auto &char_19 = char_7;
  function(char_14, char_4);
  auto &char_20 = char_14;
  char_4 = 't';
  auto char_22 = char_10;
  print("{}{}{}{}{}",
        char_1, char_7, char_4, char_22, char_16);
}

// Answer (9):
```

```
// __ __ __ __ __ __ __ __ __
```

Puzzle 82
```
auto function(char &parameter_1, char parameter_2) {
  parameter_1 = 'l';
  print("{}",
        parameter_1);
  parameter_2 = 'u';
  char char_3{'g'};
  auto &char_4 = parameter_1;
  char char_5{'e'};
  print("{}{}",
        char_5, char_3);
}
void run() {
  char char_1{'l'};
  char_1 = 'k';
  char char_3{'g'};
  char_1 = 'l';
  function(char_1, char_3);
  char char_5{'e'};
  auto char_6 = char_1;
  char char_7{'l'};
  char_6 = 'm';
  char char_9{'d'};
  auto char_10 = char_3;
  char char_11{'n'};
  auto char_12 = char_1;
  auto &char_13 = char_11;
  char_6 = 'r';
  char char_15{'q'};
  auto &char_16 = char_3;
  auto char_17 = char_5;
  char char_18{'k'};
  print("{}{}{}{}{}",
        char_5, char_11, char_9, char_6, char_17);
}

// Answer (8):

// __ __ __ __ __ __ __ __
```

Puzzle 83

```cpp
auto function(char &parameter_1, char &parameter_2) {
  parameter_1 = 'c';
  parameter_1 = '.';
  char char_3{'p'};
  auto &char_4 = char_3;
  print("{}",
        char_3);
  char char_5{'x'};
  print("{}{}",
        char_4, parameter_1);
}
void run() {
  char char_1{'c'};
  print("{}",
        char_1);
  char_1 = '.';
  auto char_3 = char_1;
  char_3 = 'b';
  function(char_1, char_3);
  auto &char_5 = char_3;
  char char_6{'k'};
  char_1 = 'r';
  auto char_8 = char_5;
  char char_9{'b'};
  auto char_10 = char_8;
  char_8 = 'e';
  char char_12{'r'};
  char_9 = 'o';
  auto char_14 = char_9;
  char char_15{'i'};
  char_15 = 'n';
  auto char_17 = char_1;
  auto &char_18 = char_8;
  auto char_19 = char_17;
  char char_20{'q'};
  auto &char_21 = char_12;
  print("{}{}{}{}{}",
        char_18, char_21, char_12, char_9, char_17);
}

// Answer (9):
```

```
// __ __ __ __ __ __ __ __ __
```

Puzzle 84

```cpp
auto function(char parameter_1, char &parameter_2) {
  parameter_2 = 's';
  print("{}",
        parameter_2);
  char char_2{'t'};
  auto &char_3 = char_2;
  char char_4{'a'};
  parameter_2 = 'n';
  print("{}",
        char_3);
}
void run() {
  char char_1{'s'};
  print("{}",
        char_1);
  char char_2{'t'};
  auto &char_3 = char_2;
  char_2 = 'a';
  auto char_5 = char_3;
  auto &char_6 = char_5;
  char_6 = 'e';
  char char_8{'m'};
  auto char_9 = char_1;
  char char_10{'r'};
  char_5 = 's';
  auto char_12 = char_6;
  char char_13{'y'};
  auto &char_14 = char_12;
  auto char_15 = char_12;
  char char_16{'e'};
  char_6 = '.';
  auto char_18 = char_5;
  function(char_9, char_15);
  char_18 = 'u';
  auto char_20 = char_13;
  print("{}{}{}{}{}{}{}{}",
        char_10, char_16, char_3, char_8, char_5, char_9,
        char_20, char_15);
```

```
}

// Answer (11):

// __ __ __ __ __ __ __ __ __ __ __
```

Puzzle 85

```cpp
auto function(char &parameter_1, char parameter_2) {
  parameter_1 = 'j';
  parameter_1 = 'b';
  char char_3{'f'};
  auto &char_4 = parameter_2;
  parameter_1 = 'p';
  auto char_6 = char_4;
  print("{}",
        char_6);
}
void run() {
  char char_1{'w'};
  auto &char_2 = char_1;
  char_1 = 'f';
  function(char_2, char_1);
  char_1 = 'e';
  auto char_5 = char_1;
  char char_6{'c'};
  print("{}",
        char_1);
  auto &char_7 = char_6;
  char_5 = 'u';
  auto &char_9 = char_1;
  function(char_2, char_5);
  char_7 = 'e';
  char char_11{'f'};
  function(char_11, char_2);
  char_2 = 'd';
  function(char_11, char_1);
  auto char_13 = char_7;
  char char_14{'n'};
  char_5 = 'a';
  auto char_16 = char_1;
  function(char_16, char_5);
  auto &char_17 = char_1;
```

```cpp
  char char_18{'t'};
  auto &char_19 = char_2;
  auto char_20 = char_9;
  char_9 = 'v';
  char char_22{'i'};
  print("{}{}{}{}{}",
        char_18, char_6, char_7, char_14, char_9);
}

// Answer (11):

// __ __ __ __ __ __ __ __ __ __ __
```

Puzzle 86

```cpp
auto function(char parameter_1, char &parameter_2) {
  char char_1{'o'};
  auto char_2 = parameter_1;
  auto &char_3 = parameter_1;
  auto char_4 = char_1;
  char char_5{'u'};
  auto char_6 = char_2;
  print("{}{}{}",
        char_3, char_4, char_6);
}
void run() {
  char char_1{'o'};
  char char_2{'.'};
  char_1 = 'w';
  auto &char_4 = char_2;
  auto char_5 = char_2;
  auto &char_6 = char_2;
  char char_7{'p'};
  auto &char_8 = char_6;
  function(char_7, char_2);
  char_5 = 'e';
  auto &char_10 = char_1;
  char_1 = 'b';
  auto char_12 = char_6;
  char_1 = 'h';
  auto &char_14 = char_2;
  auto char_15 = char_10;
  char char_16{'w'};
```

```cpp
  auto char_17 = char_8;
  char char_18{'a'};
  char_16 = 'b';
  auto char_20 = char_4;
  print("{}{}{}{}{}",
        char_12, char_1, char_5, char_18, char_7);
}

// Answer (8):

// __ __ __ __ __ __ __ __
```

Puzzle 87

```cpp
auto function(char &parameter_1, char parameter_2) {
  parameter_1 = 'j';
  char char_2{'x'};
  parameter_1 = 'f';
  auto char_4 = char_2;
  parameter_1 = 'm';
  char char_6{'c'};
  print("{}{}",
        char_6, parameter_2);
}
void run() {
  char char_1{'b'};
  auto char_2 = char_1;
  char char_3{'t'};
  char_2 = 'e';
  auto char_5 = char_2;
  char_3 = 'c';
  auto char_7 = char_5;
  char_5 = 'o';
  char char_9{'y'};
  auto &char_10 = char_7;
  char_3 = 'r';
  auto char_12 = char_3;
  char_3 = 'n';
  char char_14{'t'};
  auto &char_15 = char_12;
  char char_16{'i'};
  function(char_1, char_5);
  auto char_17 = char_12;
```

```
  auto &char_18 = char_14;
  char char_19{'i'};
  auto &char_20 = char_2;
  char char_21{'u'};
  print("{}{}{}{}{}{}{}",
        char_15, char_5, char_21, char_14, char_16, char_3,
        char_2);
}

// Answer (9):

// __ __ __ __ __ __ __ __ __
```

Puzzle 88

```
auto function(char &parameter_1, char parameter_2) {
  parameter_1 = 'e';
  char char_2{'e'};
  auto &char_3 = char_2;
  auto char_4 = char_2;
  char char_5{'u'};
  auto char_6 = char_5;
  print("{}{}{}",
        parameter_2, parameter_1, char_2);
}
void run() {
  char char_1{'e'};
  auto &char_2 = char_1;
  auto char_3 = char_1;
  char_1 = 's';
  auto char_5 = char_3;
  auto &char_6 = char_5;
  char_6 = 'y';
  auto char_8 = char_2;
  auto &char_9 = char_1;
  auto char_10 = char_2;
  char char_11{'f'};
  function(char_1, char_8);
  auto char_12 = char_1;
  char_5 = 'u';
  auto char_14 = char_2;
  char char_15{'_'};
  auto &char_16 = char_11;
```

```cpp
  char_1 = 'q';
  char char_18{'v'};
  char_5 = 'd';
  auto &char_20 = char_16;
  char_18 = 's';
  char char_22{'i'};
  print("{}{}{}{}{}",
        char_6, char_15, char_18, char_12, char_2);
}

// Answer (8):

// __ __ __ __ __ __ __ __
```

Puzzle 89

```cpp
auto function(char &parameter_1, char parameter_2) {
  parameter_1 = 's';
  parameter_2 = 'c';
  print("{}",
        parameter_2);
  char char_3{'l'};
  auto &char_4 = parameter_2;
  char_4 = 'l';
  print("{}",
        char_3);
}
void run() {
  char char_1{'s'};
  auto char_2 = char_1;
  char_1 = 'l';
  auto char_4 = char_1;
  char_4 = 'y';
  auto &char_6 = char_4;
  char char_7{'a'};
  auto char_8 = char_7;
  char char_9{'x'};
  char_6 = 'f';
  auto &char_11 = char_6;
  function(char_4, char_9);
  char char_12{'l'};
  auto char_13 = char_6;
  char_12 = 'e';
```

```cpp
  auto char_15 = char_6;
  char char_16{'q'};
  auto char_17 = char_16;
  auto &char_18 = char_17;
  char_17 = '.';
  auto char_20 = char_16;
  char char_21{'s'};
  print("{}{}{}{}{}{}",
        char_8, char_2, char_6, char_18, char_12, char_20);
}

// Answer (8):

// __ __ __ __ __ __ __ __
```

Puzzle 90

```cpp
auto function(char &parameter_1, char parameter_2) {
  char char_1{'f'};
  char_1 = 'e';
  print("{}",
        parameter_2);
  parameter_1 = 'd';
  auto char_4 = parameter_1;
  char char_5{'u'};
  print("{}",
        char_4);
}
void run() {
  char char_1{'y'};
  char_1 = 'e';
  auto &char_3 = char_1;
  auto char_4 = char_1;
  char_1 = 'u';
  char char_6{'q'};
  auto char_7 = char_4;
  print("{}",
        char_6);
  auto &char_8 = char_4;
  print("{}{}",
        char_1, char_4);
  auto char_9 = char_8;
  print("{}{}",
```

```
        char_3, char_7);
  auto &char_10 = char_4;
  auto char_11 = char_9;
  char_6 = '.';
  auto char_13 = char_9;
  char_10 = 'n';
  auto &char_15 = char_9;
  function(char_1, char_6);
  char char_16{'o'};
  char_6 = 's';
  auto &char_18 = char_4;
  char char_19{'k'};
  auto char_20 = char_19;
  char char_21{'f'};
  print("{}{}{}",
        char_11, char_21, char_18);
}


// Answer (10):


// __ __ __ __ __ __ __ __ __ __
```

Puzzle 91

```
auto function(char &parameter_1, char &parameter_2) {
  char char_1{'m'};
  auto char_2 = parameter_1;
  parameter_1 = 'n';
  char char_4{'i'};
  print("{}",
        char_1);
  char char_5{'e'};
  print("{}",
        char_5);
}
void run() {
  char char_1{'m'};
  auto &char_2 = char_1;
  char_1 = 'n';
  auto char_4 = char_2;
  char_1 = 'e';
  char char_6{'r'};
  auto &char_7 = char_4;
```

```
  auto char_8 = char_6;
  auto &char_9 = char_6;
  char char_10{'r'};
  auto &char_11 = char_7;
  char char_12{'s'};
  function(char_6, char_9);
  char char_13{'v'};
  auto &char_14 = char_8;
  auto char_15 = char_7;
  auto &char_16 = char_6;
  char_15 = 'i';
  auto char_18 = char_2;
  char char_19{'g'};
  auto char_20 = char_1;
  print("{}{}{}{}{}{}",
        char_8, char_12, char_2, char_16, char_6, char_20);
}

// Answer (8):

// __ __ __ __ __ __ __ __
```

Puzzle 92

```
auto function(char parameter_1, char &parameter_2) {
  char char_1{'q'};
  auto char_2 = parameter_1;
  parameter_2 = 'q';
  auto char_4 = char_2;
  char char_5{'t'};
  auto char_6 = char_1;
  print("{}{}",
        char_4, char_5);
}
void run() {
  char char_1{'o'};
  char_1 = 't';
  auto &char_3 = char_1;
  char_1 = 's';
  auto char_5 = char_3;
  function(char_3, char_1);
  char char_6{'m'};
  auto &char_7 = char_5;
```

```cpp
  function(char_6, char_3);
  auto &char_8 = char_3;
  char_3 = '.';
  auto char_10 = char_6;
  auto &char_11 = char_8;
  char char_12{'k'};
  char_7 = 'u';
  auto &char_14 = char_6;
  char char_15{'p'};
  auto char_16 = char_7;
  char char_17{'o'};
  char_17 = 'i';
  auto char_19 = char_16;
  char char_20{'n'};
  char_16 = 'j';
  auto char_22 = char_15;
  auto &char_23 = char_1;
  print("{}{}{}{}{}",
        char_11, char_16, char_5, char_10, char_22);
}

// Answer (9):

// __ __ __ __ __ __ __ __ __
```

Puzzle 93

```cpp
auto function(char parameter_1, char &parameter_2) {
  char char_1{'c'};
  parameter_2 = 'l';
  auto char_3 = parameter_1;
  print("{}{}",
        char_1, parameter_2);
  char_1 = 'e';
  char char_5{'b'};
  print("{}",
        parameter_1);
}
void run() {
  char char_1{'c'};
  char_1 = 'l';
  char char_3{'e'};
  char_1 = 'h';
```

```
  function(char_3, char_1);
  char char_5{'k'};
  auto &char_6 = char_5;
  char_5 = 'x';
  char char_8{'f'};
  char_6 = 'k';
  char char_10{'c'};
  auto &char_11 = char_5;
  char_5 = 't';
  auto char_13 = char_8;
  char_10 = 'r';
  char char_15{'v'};
  char_5 = 'r';
  char char_17{'y'};
  auto char_18 = char_3;
  char char_19{'a'};
  auto char_20 = char_5;
  char char_21{'j'};
  auto &char_22 = char_15;
  auto char_23 = char_11;
  char_17 = 'r';
  auto &char_25 = char_19;
  print("{}{}{}{}{}",
        char_19, char_10, char_18, char_17, char_5);
}

// Answer (8):

// __ __ __ __ __ __ __ __
```

Puzzle 94

```
auto function(char parameter_1, char &parameter_2) {
  parameter_2 = 'q';
  parameter_2 = 'u';
  print("{}",
        parameter_2);
  char char_3{'v'};
  auto &char_4 = parameter_2;
  char char_5{'e'};
  print("{}",
        char_5);
}
```

```
void run() {
  char char_1{'q'};
  char char_2{'u'};
  print("{}",
        char_1);
  auto &char_3 = char_2;
  char char_4{'o'};
  auto &char_5 = char_1;
  auto char_6 = char_4;
  char char_7{'i'};
  auto &char_8 = char_6;
  function(char_2, char_4);
  char_4 = 'o';
  auto char_10 = char_6;
  char char_11{'s'};
  auto char_12 = char_11;
  char char_13{'.'};
  char_3 = 'o';
  auto char_15 = char_11;
  function(char_3, char_7);
  char_7 = 'c';
  char char_17{'c'};
  auto &char_18 = char_2;
  char char_19{'n'};
  char_5 = 'x';
  auto char_21 = char_15;
  print("{}{}{}{}{}",
        char_13, char_17, char_2, char_19, char_11);
}

// Answer (10):

// __ __ __ __ __ __ __ __ __ __
```

Puzzle 95

```cpp
auto function(char &parameter_1, char parameter_2) {
  parameter_1 = 'h';
  char char_2{'r'};
  parameter_2 = 'e';
  auto char_4 = parameter_2;
  char char_5{'a'};
  parameter_1 = 'g';
  print("{}{}",
        char_2, parameter_2);
}
void run() {
  char char_1{'a'};
  char_1 = 'r';
  auto char_3 = char_1;
  char char_4{'y'};
  char_1 = 'a';
  auto &char_6 = char_4;
  auto char_7 = char_3;
  char char_8{'m'};
  auto char_9 = char_4;
  char_9 = 'e';
  auto char_11 = char_8;
  char char_12{'.'};
  auto &char_13 = char_11;
  auto char_14 = char_11;
  function(char_3, char_14);
  char char_15{'l'};
  char_9 = 'a';
  auto char_17 = char_4;
  char_14 = 'r';
  auto char_19 = char_4;
  char_6 = 's';
  char char_21{'r'};
  auto &char_22 = char_3;
  char char_23{'n'};
  auto char_24 = char_22;
  print("{}{}{}{}{}{}{}{}",
        char_12, char_22, char_21, char_9, char_13, char_8,
        char_1, char_7);
}
```

```
// Answer (10):

// __ __ __ __ __ __ __ __ __ __
```

Puzzle 96

```
auto function(char &parameter_1, char parameter_2) {
  parameter_1 = 'k';
  parameter_2 = 't';
  print("{}",
        parameter_2);
  char char_3{'i'};
  auto char_4 = char_3;
  print("{}",
        char_4);
}
void run() {
  char char_1{'t'};
  char_1 = 't';
  auto char_3 = char_1;
  char char_4{'d'};
  auto char_5 = char_1;
  function(char_1, char_3);
  char char_6{'a'};
  auto &char_7 = char_3;
  char char_8{'b'};
  char_5 = 'v';
  auto &char_10 = char_4;
  auto char_11 = char_10;
  char_11 = 'e';
  auto &char_13 = char_11;
  char char_14{'s'};
  auto &char_15 = char_13;
  char char_16{'d'};
  auto &char_17 = char_1;
  auto char_18 = char_14;
  char_3 = 'm';
  auto char_20 = char_6;
  char char_21{'_'};
  auto &char_22 = char_7;
  print("{}{}{}{}{}{}{}",
        char_22, char_11, char_21, char_8, char_20, char_18,
        char_13);
```

```
}

// Answer (9):

// __ __ __ __ __ __ __ __
```

std::swap

Swap Example 1

```cpp
void run()
{
  int value = 4;
  int value2 = 2;
  print("{}{}", value, value2);
}

// Answer: 42
```

Swap Example 2

```cpp
void run()
{
  int value = 4;
  int value2 = 2;
  std::swap(value, value2);
  print("{}{}", value, value2);
}

// Answer: 24
```

char std::swap Puzzles

Puzzle 97

```cpp
void run() {
  char char_1{'n'};
  auto char_2 = char_1;
  char_2 = 'P';
  char char_4{'A'};
  auto char_5 = char_2;
  print("{}",
        char_5);
  auto &char_6 = char_5;
  char_5 = 'D';
  auto char_8 = char_5;
  print("{}{}",
        char_4, char_6);
  auto char_9 = char_6;
  char_8 = 'Q';
  auto &char_11 = char_1;
  char_6 = 'y';
  auto char_13 = char_11;
  auto &char_14 = char_4;
  print("{}{}",
        char_9, char_8);
}

// Answer (5):

// __ __ __ __ __
```

Puzzle 98

```cpp
void run() {
  char char_1{'u'};
  char_1 = 'a';
  auto &char_3 = char_1;
  auto char_4 = char_1;
  auto &char_5 = char_3;
  auto char_6 = char_1;
  char_5 = 'l';
  char char_8{'a'};
  auto &char_9 = char_6;
  auto char_10 = char_1;
  char_10 = 'C';
  auto char_12 = char_3;
  char_9 = 'e';
  print("{}{}{}{}",
        char_10, char_8, char_1, char_5);
  char char_14{'b'};
  auto char_15 = char_14;
  print("{}{}{}{}",
        char_4, char_15, char_3, char_6);
}

// Answer (8):

// __ __ __ __ __ __ __ __
```

Puzzle 99

```cpp
void run() {
  char char_1{'j'};
  auto &char_2 = char_1;
  char_1 = 'i';
  std::swap(char_2, char_1);
  auto char_4 = char_2;
  char_1 = 'f';
  auto char_6 = char_4;
  char char_7{'d'};
  std::swap(char_7, char_6);
  char char_8{'g'};
  std::swap(char_8, char_6);
  print("{}{}",
```

```cpp
        char_8, char_7);
  char_7 = 'j';
  char char_10{'p'};
  print("{}",
        char_2);
  char_6 = 'e';
  std::swap(char_8, char_6);
  print("{}",
        char_1);
  auto char_12 = char_7;
  char char_13{'e'};
  std::swap(char_7, char_2);
  char_12 = 'm';
  auto char_15 = char_7;
  char char_16{'p'};
  auto &char_17 = char_13;
  char char_18{'t'};
  print("{}{}{}{}",
        char_18, char_4, char_12, char_17);
}

// Answer (8):

// __ __ __ __ __ __ __ __
```

Puzzle 100

```cpp
void run() {
  char char_1{'e'};
  char char_2{'i'};
  auto char_3 = char_2;
  print("{}",
        char_3);
  char char_4{'e'};
  auto char_5 = char_4;
  char char_6{'s'};
  auto char_7 = char_5;
  std::swap(char_2, char_3);
  char char_8{'l'};
  char_2 = 's';
  auto char_10 = char_7;
  auto &char_11 = char_6;
  char_2 = 'e';
```

```cpp
  std::swap(char_8, char_3);
  char_5 = 'l';
  auto char_14 = char_6;
  std::swap(char_14, char_10);
  auto char_15 = char_11;
  char char_16{'l'};
  auto &char_17 = char_10;
  print("{}{}{}{}{}",
        char_10, char_16, char_4, char_17, char_15);
}

// Answer (6):

// __ __ __ __ __ __
```

Puzzle 101

```cpp
void run() {
  char char_1{'e'};
  auto char_2 = char_1;
  auto &char_3 = char_2;
  char char_4{'c'};
  char_2 = 'w';
  char char_6{'c'};
  char_1 = 't';
  auto &char_8 = char_6;
  char char_9{'w'};
  print("{}{}",
        char_9, char_6);
  char_4 = 'f';
  char char_11{'x'};
  auto &char_12 = char_1;
  char_3 = 'y';
  char char_14{'p'};
  auto char_15 = char_9;
  std::swap(char_11, char_9);
  auto &char_16 = char_14;
  char char_17{'e'};
  auto char_18 = char_9;
  auto &char_19 = char_14;
  auto char_20 = char_14;
  print("{}{}{}{}",
        char_12, char_3, char_14, char_17);
```

```cpp
}
```

```cpp
// Answer (6):
```

```cpp
// __ __ __ __ __ __
```

Puzzle 102

```cpp
void run() {
  char char_1{'s'};
  char_1 = 'x';
  char char_3{'n'};
  auto &char_4 = char_3;
  char char_5{'j'};
  auto char_6 = char_5;
  char_4 = 'e';
  auto char_8 = char_4;
  char char_9{'w'};
  char_8 = 'j';
  auto &char_11 = char_9;
  char char_12{'O'};
  char_5 = '2';
  auto &char_14 = char_6;
  char_8 = 'M';
  auto char_16 = char_8;
  char char_17{'w'};
  auto &char_18 = char_14;
  char_6 = 'V';
  auto char_20 = char_18;
  std::swap(char_1, char_5);
  char_8 = 'M';
  auto &char_22 = char_12;
  char char_23{'P'};
  char_11 = 'B';
  std::swap(char_9, char_4);
  auto char_25 = char_8;
  print("{}{}{}{}{}{}{}{}",
        char_14, char_23, char_8, char_22, char_20, char_4,
        char_1, char_16);
}
```

```cpp
// Answer (8):
```

```
// __ __ __ __ __ __ __ __
```

Puzzle 103

```cpp
void run() {
  char char_1{'D'};
  auto char_2 = char_1;
  char char_3{'d'};
  auto char_4 = char_3;
  auto &char_5 = char_3;
  char char_6{'A'};
  char_4 = 'w';
  auto &char_8 = char_1;
  char_2 = 'a';
  char char_10{'-'};
  auto &char_11 = char_2;
  auto char_12 = char_6;
  std::swap(char_1, char_8);
  auto &char_13 = char_11;
  auto char_14 = char_5;
  auto &char_15 = char_4;
  char char_16{'x'};
  char_15 = 'c';
  std::swap(char_13, char_4);
  auto &char_18 = char_15;
  auto char_19 = char_3;
  std::swap(char_1, char_18);
  char char_20{'A'};
  char_6 = 'i';
  auto char_22 = char_5;
  char char_23{'D'};
  print("{}{}{}{}{}{}{}",
        char_20, char_23, char_15, char_10, char_12, char_3,
        char_14);
}

// Answer (7):
```

```
// __ __ __ __ __ __ __ __
```

Puzzle 104

```cpp
void run() {
  char char_1{'p'};
  auto char_2 = char_1;
  auto &char_3 = char_1;
  char_2 = 'l';
  char char_5{'c'};
  char_1 = 'o';
  auto char_7 = char_3;
  char char_8{'p'};
  char_8 = 't';
  auto &char_10 = char_2;
  char_7 = '_';
  char char_12{'m'};
  auto &char_13 = char_7;
  char char_14{'y'};
  char_2 = 'm';
  print("{}{}{}{}{}",
        char_5, char_3, char_12, char_2, char_1);
  char char_16{'d'};
  char_16 = 'd';
  std::swap(char_13, char_7);
  char_1 = 'p';
  auto char_19 = char_8;
  char char_20{'n'};
  auto char_21 = char_13;
  auto &char_22 = char_1;
  char char_23{'t'};
  print("{}{}{}{}",
        char_20, char_13, char_19, char_14);
  std::swap(char_10, char_3);
  char char_24{'y'};
  auto &char_25 = char_7;
  char char_26{'e'};
  char_1 = 'c';
  auto char_28 = char_10;
  print("{}{}{}{}",
        char_28, char_26, char_7, char_23);
}

// Answer (13):
```

```
// __ __ __ __ __ __ __ __ __ __ __ __ __ __
```

Puzzle 105

```cpp
auto function(char &parameter_1, char parameter_2) {
  parameter_1 = 'f';
  parameter_2 = 'a';
  char char_3{'s'};
  print("{}",
        char_3);
  auto &char_4 = char_3;
  char char_5{'m'};
  print("{}",
        parameter_2);
}
void run() {
  char char_1{'o'};
  auto char_2 = char_1;
  char char_3{'s'};
  auto char_4 = char_1;
  char_4 = 'm';
  char char_6{'l'};
  auto &char_7 = char_1;
  char char_8{'j'};
  auto &char_9 = char_2;
  char_7 = 'p';
  function(char_3, char_8);
  char char_11{'e'};
  auto &char_12 = char_3;
  print("{}{}{}{}",
        char_4, char_7, char_6, char_11);
}

// Answer (6):

// __ __ __ __ __ __ __
```

Puzzle 106

```cpp
auto function(char &parameter_1, char parameter_2) {
  print("{}",
        parameter_1);
  parameter_2 = 'O';
  char char_2{'U'};
  auto &char_3 = char_2;
  parameter_1 = 'x';
  char char_5{'r'};
  print("{}",
        char_3);
}
void run() {
  char char_1{'O'};
  auto char_2 = char_1;
  char char_3{'W'};
  auto &char_4 = char_1;
  char_2 = 'y';
  std::swap(char_2, char_1);
  function(char_2, char_3);
  auto &char_6 = char_4;
  char_4 = 'T';
  auto &char_8 = char_6;
  char char_9{'S'};
  auto char_10 = char_3;
  auto &char_11 = char_1;
  std::swap(char_9, char_8);
  auto &char_12 = char_9;
  print("{}{}{}",
        char_9, char_6, char_3);
}


// Answer (5):

// __ __ __ __ __
```

Puzzle 107

```cpp
auto function(char &parameter_1, char &parameter_2) {
  parameter_1 = 'l';
  parameter_2 = 'm';
  print("{}",
        parameter_2);
  parameter_1 = 'e';
  std::swap(parameter_2, parameter_1);
  char char_4{'a'};
  print("{}",
        char_4);
}
void run() {
  char char_1{'h'};
  auto &char_2 = char_1;
  auto char_3 = char_1;
  std::swap(char_1, char_3);
  char_1 = 'a';
  char char_5{'F'};
  auto &char_6 = char_2;
  char_1 = 'o';
  char char_8{'r'};
  auto &char_9 = char_6;
  print("{}{}{}",
        char_5, char_6, char_8);
  function(char_9, char_6);
  auto char_10 = char_6;
  char char_11{'e'};
  auto &char_12 = char_11;
  std::swap(char_8, char_2);
  char_11 = 't';
  auto &char_14 = char_9;
  print("{}{}{}{}",
        char_11, char_12, char_10, char_2);
}

// Answer (9):

// __ __ __ __ __ __ __ __ __
```

Puzzle 108

```cpp
auto function(char parameter_1, char &parameter_2) {
  char char_1{'p'};
  parameter_2 = '.';
  char char_3{'t'};
  auto char_4 = parameter_1;
  char char_5{'e'};
  char_1 = 'p';
  print("{}{}",
        char_3, char_5);
}
void run() {
  char char_1{'q'};
  auto &char_2 = char_1;
  char_2 = 't';
  std::swap(char_1, char_2);
  char char_4{'m'};
  function(char_1, char_2);
  std::swap(char_4, char_2);
  auto char_5 = char_4;
  char char_6{'p'};
  auto &char_7 = char_1;
  auto char_8 = char_1;
  char_8 = 'r';
  char char_10{'p'};
  auto &char_11 = char_6;
  print("{}{}{}{}",
        char_1, char_10, char_4, char_6);
  char_11 = 'w';
  auto &char_13 = char_6;
  char_13 = 'a';
  auto &char_15 = char_13;
  print("{}{}{}{}",
        char_13, char_8, char_11, char_2);
}

// Answer (10):

// __ __ __ __ __ __ __ __ __ __
```

Puzzle 109

```
auto function(char parameter_1, char &parameter_2) {
  parameter_2 = 'P';
  parameter_2 = 'W';
  char char_3{'o'};
  char_3 = 'j';
  auto char_5 = char_3;
  std::swap(parameter_1, char_3);
  print("{}",
        char_3);
}
void run() {
  char char_1{'P'};
  auto &char_2 = char_1;
  auto char_3 = char_1;
  char char_4{'d'};
  char_4 = 'S';
  print("{}",
        char_3);
  char char_6{'o'};
  function(char_4, char_3);
  char char_7{'k'};
  char_1 = 'U';
  auto char_9 = char_1;
  function(char_2, char_6);
  char char_10{'B'};
  auto char_11 = char_10;
  char char_12{'g'};
  auto &char_13 = char_9;
  char char_14{'U'};
  print("{}{}{}{}",
        char_10, char_14, char_4, char_6);
}

// Answer (7):

// __ __ __ __ __ __ __
```

Puzzle 110

```cpp
auto function(char parameter_1, char &parameter_2) {
  parameter_2 = 'l';
  std::swap(parameter_2, parameter_1);
  parameter_2 = 'f';
  char char_3{'r'};
  auto &char_4 = char_3;
  auto char_5 = parameter_2;
  print("{}",
        char_3);
}
void run() {
  char char_1{'t'};
  auto char_2 = char_1;
  char_2 = 'r';
  auto &char_4 = char_1;
  auto char_5 = char_4;
  function(char_1, char_2);
  auto &char_6 = char_5;
  char char_7{'x'};
  char_6 = 'e';
  auto char_9 = char_1;
  char_4 = 'e';
  auto &char_11 = char_6;
  print("{}{}{}",
        char_6, char_2, char_1);
  function(char_7, char_6);
  auto char_12 = char_4;
  char_5 = 'c';
  char char_14{'n'};
  auto &char_15 = char_6;
  char_9 = 'k';
  char char_17{'e'};
  print("{}{}{}{}",
        char_17, char_14, char_5, char_12);
}

// Answer (9):

// __ __ __ __ __ __ __ __ __ __
```

Puzzle 111

```cpp
auto function(char &parameter_1, char parameter_2) {
  parameter_2 = 'c';
  char char_2{'u'};
  auto &char_3 = parameter_2;
  parameter_2 = '.';
  char char_5{'s'};
  auto char_6 = char_5;
  print("{}{}{}",
        char_5, char_6, parameter_2);
}
void run() {
  char char_1{'c'};
  char char_2{'q'};
  char_2 = 'a';
  print("{}",
        char_1);
  std::swap(char_2, char_1);
  char char_4{'.'};
  char_2 = 's';
  auto &char_6 = char_1;
  char_2 = 'l';
  print("{}{}",
        char_2, char_6);
  char char_8{'g'};
  auto char_9 = char_8;
  std::swap(char_2, char_1);
  char char_10{'h'};
  char_2 = 's';
  auto char_12 = char_1;
  char_10 = 'c';
  auto &char_14 = char_1;
  std::swap(char_10, char_9);
  char char_15{'e'};
  auto &char_16 = char_2;
  function(char_15, char_14);
  auto &char_17 = char_8;
  char char_18{'i'};
  print("{}{}{}{}{}{}",
        char_17, char_16, char_12, char_18, char_9, char_15);
}
```

```cpp
// Answer (12):

// __ __ __ __ __ __ __ __ __ __ __ __
```

Puzzle 112

```cpp
auto function(char &parameter_1, char &parameter_2) {
  char char_1{'c'};
  auto char_2 = char_1;
  auto &char_3 = char_2;
  char_3 = 'd';
  auto &char_5 = char_2;
  auto char_6 = char_5;
  print("{}{}",
        char_3, parameter_2);
}
void run() {
  char char_1{'c'};
  auto char_2 = char_1;
  auto &char_3 = char_1;
  function(char_3, char_2);
  auto &char_4 = char_2;
  char char_5{'f'};
  auto char_6 = char_3;
  auto &char_7 = char_2;
  auto char_8 = char_6;
  char char_9{'v'};
  char_6 = 'd';
  auto &char_11 = char_7;
  char char_12{'c'};
  char_2 = 'l';
  auto &char_14 = char_3;
  char_5 = '.';
  char char_16{'q'};
  print("{}{}{}{}{}",
        char_7, char_5, char_6, char_3, char_4);
}

// Answer (7):

// __ __ __ __ __ __ __
```

Puzzle 113

```cpp
auto function(char parameter_1, char &parameter_2) {
  parameter_1 = 'd';
  parameter_2 = 'v';
  char char_3{'a'};
  parameter_1 = 'i';
  char char_5{'p'};
  print("{}{}",
        parameter_2, char_3);
}
void run() {
  char char_1{'d'};
  auto char_2 = char_1;
  char_2 = 'a';
  auto &char_4 = char_2;
  print("{}{}",
        char_4, char_1);
  auto &char_5 = char_2;
  char char_6{'s'};
  auto &char_7 = char_5;
  char_5 = 'k';
  auto &char_9 = char_4;
  char_9 = 'c';
  char char_11{'y'};
  char_6 = 'e';
  function(char_5, char_4);
  char char_13{'a'};
  char_2 = 'c';
  auto char_15 = char_9;
  char char_16{'n'};
  auto char_17 = char_9;
  auto &char_18 = char_17;
  print("{}{}{}",
        char_16, char_7, char_6);
}

// Answer (7):

// __ __ __ __ __ __ __
```

Puzzle 114

```cpp
auto function(char &parameter_1, char &parameter_2) {
  char char_1{'g'};
  print("{}{}",
        parameter_2, char_1);
  auto char_2 = parameter_2;
  parameter_2 = 'j';
  char char_4{'u'};
  print("{}{}",
        char_4, parameter_1);
}
void run() {
  char char_1{'g'};
  char_1 = 'l';
  char char_3{'k'};
  print("{}",
        char_1);
  auto &char_4 = char_3;
  char_3 = 'e';
  auto char_6 = char_4;
  char_1 = 'a';
  function(char_6, char_1);
  char_6 = 'l';
  auto &char_9 = char_1;
  char_9 = 'r';
  auto char_11 = char_3;
  std::swap(char_4, char_1);
  auto char_12 = char_9;
  char_12 = 'e';
  auto char_14 = char_4;
  auto &char_15 = char_14;
  auto char_16 = char_11;
  char char_17{'x'};
  auto &char_18 = char_17;
  std::swap(char_17, char_4);
  auto &char_19 = char_12;
  auto char_20 = char_3;
  print("{}{}{}{}",
        char_17, char_15, char_12, char_6);
}

// Answer (9):
```

```cpp
// __ __ __ __ __ __ __ __ __
```

Puzzle 115

```cpp
auto function(char &parameter_1, char parameter_2) {
  std::swap(parameter_1, parameter_2);
  parameter_1 = 'e';
  char char_2{'x'};
  auto char_3 = parameter_1;
  auto &char_4 = char_3;
  char_3 = 'p';
  print("{}{}",
        parameter_1, char_2);
}
void run() {
  char char_1{'e'};
  auto char_2 = char_1;
  auto &char_3 = char_1;
  auto char_4 = char_3;
  char char_5{'p'};
  char_1 = 'q';
  char char_7{'c'};
  char_3 = 'q';
  std::swap(char_5, char_1);
  auto char_9 = char_3;
  char_4 = '.';
  auto char_11 = char_4;
  char char_12{'r'};
  char_1 = 'd';
  function(char_1, char_7);
  auto char_14 = char_12;
  char char_15{'j'};
  auto char_16 = char_4;
  auto &char_17 = char_9;
  char_16 = 'f';
  auto char_19 = char_14;
  print("{}{}{}{}{}{}",
        char_9, char_14, char_11, char_17, char_12, char_2);
}

// Answer (8):
```

```
// __ __ __ __ __ __ __ __
```

Puzzle 116

```cpp
auto function(char parameter_1, char &parameter_2) {
  parameter_1 = 'e';
  print("{}",
        parameter_2);
  parameter_1 = 'l';
  print("{}",
        parameter_1);
  std::swap(parameter_2, parameter_1);
  parameter_2 = 'c';
}
void run() {
  char char_1{'e'};
  print("{}",
        char_1);
  char_1 = 'l';
  auto char_3 = char_1;
  auto &char_4 = char_1;
  char_4 = 'r';
  char char_6{'g'};
  char_6 = 'v';
  auto &char_8 = char_4;
  char_8 = 'l';
  auto &char_10 = char_1;
  function(char_10, char_4);
  auto char_11 = char_4;
  auto &char_12 = char_4;
  char char_13{'_'};
  auto &char_14 = char_8;
  char char_15{'2'};
  auto char_16 = char_6;
  char_12 = 't';
  char char_18{'n'};
  std::swap(char_12, char_15);
  auto char_19 = char_15;
  char char_20{'i'};
  print("{}{}{}{}{}{}",
        char_20, char_18, char_15, char_13, char_4, char_3);
}
```

```
// Answer (9):

// __ __ __ __ __ __ __ __ __
```

Puzzle 117

```cpp
auto function(char &parameter_1, char parameter_2) {
  parameter_2 = 's';
  print("{}",
        parameter_1);
  parameter_1 = 'u';
  char char_3{'x'};
  char_3 = 't';
  auto &char_5 = char_3;
  print("{}",
        char_3);
}
void run() {
  char char_1{'s'};
  auto char_2 = char_1;
  char char_3{'x'};
  function(char_1, char_2);
  auto &char_4 = char_1;
  char_2 = 'r';
  function(char_2, char_4);
  auto &char_6 = char_2;
  char char_7{'a'};
  std::swap(char_1, char_7);
  auto &char_8 = char_7;
  auto char_9 = char_3;
  char_7 = 'o';
  char char_11{'y'};
  auto char_12 = char_8;
  auto &char_13 = char_6;
  char char_14{'m'};
  char_11 = 'v';
  auto &char_16 = char_7;
  auto char_17 = char_12;
  char char_18{'k'};
  print("{}{}{}{}{}",
        char_12, char_6, char_14, char_4, char_9);
}
```

```cpp
// Answer (9):

// __ __ __ __ __ __ __ __ __
```

Puzzle 118

```cpp
auto function(char &parameter_1, char parameter_2) {
  char char_1{'k'};
  parameter_2 = 'f';
  auto char_3 = parameter_1;
  std::swap(char_3, parameter_2);
  parameter_2 = 'n';
  char char_5{'l'};
  print("{}",
        char_5);
}
void run() {
  char char_1{'p'};
  auto &char_2 = char_1;
  char char_3{'s'};
  auto &char_4 = char_1;
  auto char_5 = char_4;
  auto &char_6 = char_3;
  char char_7{'o'};
  char_3 = 'd';
  function(char_5, char_4);
  char char_9{'u'};
  auto &char_10 = char_1;
  std::swap(char_1, char_5);
  char char_11{'t'};
  auto char_12 = char_6;
  char_4 = 'n';
  char char_14{'w'};
  function(char_7, char_1);
  auto char_15 = char_3;
  std::swap(char_4, char_3);
  char char_16{'r'};
  auto char_17 = char_16;
  auto &char_18 = char_3;
  print("{}{}{}{}{}",
        char_17, char_7, char_9, char_18, char_2);
}
```

```cpp
// Answer (7):

// __ __ __ __ __ __ __
```

Puzzle 119

```cpp
auto function(char &parameter_1, char &parameter_2) {
  print("{}",
        parameter_1);
  char char_1{'u'};
  parameter_1 = 's';
  auto &char_3 = char_1;
  auto char_4 = char_1;
  auto &char_5 = parameter_1;
  print("{}",
        char_4);
}
void run() {
  char char_1{'u'};
  char_1 = 's';
  auto &char_3 = char_1;
  auto char_4 = char_1;
  char char_5{'t'};
  char_4 = 'f';
  function(char_4, char_5);
  auto &char_7 = char_5;
  auto char_8 = char_7;
  char char_9{'q'};
  auto char_10 = char_5;
  auto &char_11 = char_7;
  char char_12{'a'};
  char_5 = '.';
  function(char_10, char_3);
  char char_14{'t'};
  std::swap(char_1, char_4);
  char_9 = 'k';
  auto &char_16 = char_7;
  std::swap(char_3, char_5);
  auto &char_17 = char_3;
  std::swap(char_17, char_12);
  char_4 = 'a';
  char char_19{'b'};
```

```cpp
  char_19 = 'r';
  auto char_21 = char_7;
  char char_22{'e'};
  print("{}{}{}{}{}{}{}{}",
        char_19, char_22, char_10, char_12, char_14, char_17,
        char_16, char_9);
}

// Answer (12):

// __ __ __ __ __ __ __ __ __ __ __ __
```

Puzzle 120

```cpp
auto function(char &parameter_1, char parameter_2) {
  std::swap(parameter_1, parameter_2);
  char char_1{'r'};
  auto &char_2 = char_1;
  std::swap(parameter_2, char_2);
  parameter_1 = 'o';
  char char_4{'j'};
  print("{}",
        char_2);
}
void run() {
  char char_1{'c'};
  char_1 = 'v';
  char_1 = 'o';
  char char_4{'k'};
  char_1 = 'c';
  function(char_1, char_4);
  char_1 = 'r';
  char char_7{':'};
  char_4 = 'h';
  auto &char_9 = char_4;
  char char_10{'o'};
  function(char_9, char_10);
  char_4 = 'd';
  char char_12{':'};
  auto char_13 = char_12;
  char char_14{'t'};
  function(char_1, char_7);
  char_14 = 'g';
```

```cpp
    std::swap(char_4, char_14);
    auto &char_16 = char_10;
    char_14 = 'f';
    auto char_18 = char_14;
    auto &char_19 = char_9;
    std::swap(char_12, char_14);
    auto &char_20 = char_18;
    std::swap(char_9, char_19);
    auto char_21 = char_1;
    char char_22{'j'};
    char_9 = 'l';
    function(char_10, char_19);
    char char_24{'n'};
    char_20 = 'i';
    std::swap(char_1, char_18);
    char char_26{'f'};
    function(char_24, char_16);
    char_20 = 'r';
    function(char_24, char_26);
    auto char_28 = char_7;
    print("{}{}{}{}{}{}{}",
          char_13, char_7, char_12, char_19, char_21, char_10,
          char_18);
}

// Answer (13):

// __ __ __ __ __ __ __ __ __ __ __ __ __
```

Puzzle 121

```cpp
auto function(char &parameter_1, char &parameter_2) {
    parameter_2 = 'c';
    parameter_1 = 'q';
    char char_3{'l'};
    auto &char_4 = char_3;
    std::swap(char_3, parameter_2);
    auto &char_5 = parameter_2;
    print("{}",
          char_4);
}
void run() {
    char char_1{'c'};
```

```cpp
    char char_2{'i'};
    char_1 = 'l';
    auto &char_4 = char_2;
    char_4 = 'a';
    print("{}",
          char_4);
    auto char_6 = char_1;
    char char_7{'m'};
    function(char_1, char_4);
    auto char_8 = char_7;
    char char_9{'l'};
    auto char_10 = char_9;
    char char_11{'a'};
    std::swap(char_4, char_10);
    char_9 = 't';
    char char_13{'u'};
    function(char_1, char_2);
    char char_14{'s'};
    auto char_15 = char_8;
    char char_16{'w'};
    char_14 = 'e';
    auto &char_18 = char_2;
    char char_19{'e'};
    char_6 = 'e';
    auto &char_21 = char_19;
    char_1 = 'u';
    auto &char_23 = char_13;
    print("{}{}{}{}{}{}{}",
          char_13, char_8, char_1, char_18, char_11, char_9,
          char_21);
}

// Answer (10):

// ___ ___ ___ ___ ___ ___ ___ ___ ___ ___
```

Puzzle 122

```cpp
auto function(char &parameter_1, char &parameter_2) {
  parameter_2 = 'd';
  print("{}",
        parameter_1);
  char char_2{'b'};
  auto &char_3 = char_2;
  char char_4{'.'};
  auto &char_5 = parameter_2;
  print("{}{}",
        parameter_2, char_4);
}
void run() {
  char char_1{'d'};
  char char_2{'b'};
  print("{}",
        char_2);
  char char_3{'a'};
  auto char_4 = char_1;
  std::swap(char_3, char_1);
  char char_5{'l'};
  auto char_6 = char_3;
  auto &char_7 = char_5;
  auto char_8 = char_5;
  std::swap(char_4, char_8);
  char char_9{'p'};
  auto char_10 = char_7;
  char char_11{'c'};
  function(char_1, char_2);
  auto &char_12 = char_9;
  char char_13{'k'};
  char_2 = 's';
  auto char_15 = char_8;
  auto &char_16 = char_1;
  auto char_17 = char_12;
  char_12 = 'o';
  char char_19{'c'};
  print("{}{}{}{}{}",
        char_16, char_10, char_7, char_12, char_19);
}

// Answer (9):
```

```
// _ __ __ __ __ __ __ __ __
```

Puzzle 123

```cpp
auto function(char &parameter_1, char parameter_2) {
  char char_1{'g'};
  char char_2{'F'};
  char_1 = 'S';
  auto char_4 = char_2;
  auto &char_5 = char_1;
  char char_6{'T'};
  print("{}{}",
        char_4, char_6);
}
void run() {
  char char_1{'k'};
  auto char_2 = char_1;
  char_1 = 'S';
  auto &char_4 = char_1;
  char_2 = 'E';
  char char_6{'T'};
  char_6 = 'u';
  auto char_8 = char_4;
  auto &char_9 = char_6;
  auto char_10 = char_8;
  char_10 = '-';
  auto char_12 = char_10;
  auto &char_13 = char_1;
  auto char_14 = char_4;
  auto &char_15 = char_8;
  char_9 = 'o';
  char char_17{'T'};
  char_8 = 'f';
  auto char_19 = char_12;
  function(char_17, char_14);
  auto char_20 = char_1;
  char char_21{'T'};
  auto &char_22 = char_4;
  auto char_23 = char_21;
  char char_24{'i'};
  print("{}{}{}{}{}{}{}",
        char_4, char_23, char_19, char_21, char_2, char_13,
```

```cpp
      char_17);
}
```

```cpp
// Answer (9):
```

```cpp
// __ __ __ __ __ __ __ __ __
```

Puzzle 124

```cpp
auto function(char &parameter_1, char parameter_2) {
  parameter_1 = 'm';
  parameter_2 = 'e';
  std::swap(parameter_2, parameter_1);
  char char_3{'t'};
  print("{}{}",
        parameter_2, parameter_1);
  parameter_2 = 'w';
  print("{}",
        char_3);
}
void run() {
  char char_1{'m'};
  auto char_2 = char_1;
  auto &char_3 = char_2;
  char char_4{'e'};
  std::swap(char_3, char_4);
  char_1 = 't';
  auto &char_6 = char_1;
  function(char_4, char_1);
  char char_7{'x'};
  char_1 = 'h';
  char char_9{'s'};
  char_3 = 'e';
  auto &char_11 = char_6;
  auto char_12 = char_6;
  char char_13{'.'};
  char_12 = 'l';
  auto char_15 = char_13;
  std::swap(char_13, char_3);
  char char_16{'a'};
  auto char_17 = char_2;
  auto &char_18 = char_6;
  auto char_19 = char_2;
```

```cpp
    char_7 = 'p';
    std::swap(char_16, char_3);
    char_4 = 'i';
    auto &char_22 = char_18;
    char char_23{'s'};
    auto char_24 = char_15;
    print("{}{}{}{}{}{}",
          char_3, char_24, char_18, char_13, char_12, char_7);
}

// Answer (9):

// __ __ __ __ __ __ __ __ __
```

Puzzle 125

```cpp
auto function(char parameter_1, char &parameter_2) {
  std::swap(parameter_2, parameter_1);
  std::swap(parameter_2, parameter_1);
  parameter_1 = 'e';
  print("{}",
        parameter_1);
  char char_2{'.'};
  print("{}",
        char_2);
}
void run() {
  char char_1{'e'};
  char_1 = '.';
  auto &char_3 = char_1;
  char_1 = 'a';
  auto char_5 = char_3;
  auto &char_6 = char_3;
  char char_7{'r'};
  print("{}{}",
        char_7, char_3);
  auto &char_8 = char_7;
  char_5 = 'n';
  char char_10{'g'};
  char_3 = 'p';
  char char_12{'u'};
  char_6 = 'c';
  print("{}{}",
```

```cpp
        char_5, char_10);
  auto char_14 = char_8;
  auto &char_15 = char_5;
  auto char_16 = char_5;
  char char_17{'y'};
  auto char_18 = char_1;
  auto &char_19 = char_17;
  char char_20{'r'};
  char_3 = 'o';
  char char_22{'b'};
  char_12 = 'm';
  char char_24{'w'};
  std::swap(char_24, char_18);
  char_7 = 'r';
  function(char_3, char_16);
  auto &char_26 = char_19;
  char char_27{'e'};
  print("{}{}{}{}{}",
        char_27, char_14, char_8, char_6, char_20);
}

// Answer (11):

// __ __ __ __ __ __ __ __ __ __ __
```

Puzzle 126

```cpp
auto function(char parameter_1, char &parameter_2) {
  char char_1{'x'};
  parameter_2 = 'h';
  std::swap(parameter_1, parameter_2);
  auto char_3 = char_1;
  auto &char_4 = char_1;
  char char_5{'t'};
  print("{}{}",
        parameter_2, char_5);
}
void run() {
  char char_1{'j'};
  char_1 = 'y';
  char char_3{'l'};
  char_1 = 'a';
  char char_5{'t'};
```

```cpp
  auto char_6 = char_5;
  char char_7{'.'};
  char_5 = 's';
  auto char_9 = char_1;
  char_6 = 'q';
  auto &char_11 = char_7;
  auto char_12 = char_6;
  char char_13{'n'};
  auto &char_14 = char_9;
  function(char_5, char_3);
  std::swap(char_12, char_1);
  auto &char_15 = char_1;
  char_14 = 'c';
  char char_17{'e'};
  auto char_18 = char_5;
  char char_19{'y'};
  char_17 = 'l';
  char char_21{'l'};
  auto char_22 = char_13;
  char char_23{'e'};
  auto char_24 = char_13;
  char char_25{'k'};
  print("{}{}{}{}{}{}{}",
        char_12, char_14, char_25, char_7, char_3, char_19,
        char_13);
}

// Answer (9):

// __ __ __ __ __ __ __ __ __
```

Puzzle 127

```cpp
auto function(char &parameter_1, char parameter_2) {
  char char_1{'r'};
  parameter_2 = 'f';
  char char_3{'l'};
  auto &char_4 = parameter_1;
  std::swap(char_1, char_3);
  char_1 = 'e';
  print("{}{}",
        parameter_2, char_1);
}
```

```cpp
void run() {
  char char_1{'r'};
  auto char_2 = char_1;
  char char_3{'l'};
  auto char_4 = char_2;
  char_1 = 'e';
  auto &char_6 = char_1;
  char char_7{'c'};
  function(char_1, char_2);
  char_4 = 'q';
  char char_9{'l'};
  std::swap(char_7, char_6);
  char char_10{'g'};
  auto &char_11 = char_9;
  std::swap(char_11, char_9);
  auto char_12 = char_2;
  char_4 = 'a';
  char char_14{'x'};
  auto char_15 = char_2;
  char_14 = 'e';
  char char_17{'b'};
  auto &char_18 = char_1;
  char_12 = 'q';
  char char_20{'x'};
  char_2 = 'e';
  auto &char_22 = char_7;
  char char_23{'t'};
  char_9 = 'p';
  char char_25{'y'};
  auto char_26 = char_7;
  auto &char_27 = char_20;
  print("{}{}{}{}{}{}{}{}{}{}{}",
        char_18, char_3, char_2, char_4, char_15, char_7,
        char_27, char_1, char_14, char_9, char_23);
}


// Answer (13):

// __ __ __ __ __ __ __ __ __ __ __
```

Puzzle 128

```cpp
auto function(char &parameter_1, char &parameter_2) {
  std::swap(parameter_2, parameter_1);
  print("{}",
        parameter_1);
  parameter_1 = 'e';
  char char_2{'s'};
  auto char_3 = parameter_1;
  auto &char_4 = parameter_1;
  print("{}",
        parameter_2);
}
void run() {
  char char_1{'e'};
  auto char_2 = char_1;
  auto &char_3 = char_2;
  auto char_4 = char_3;
  char_2 = 'n';
  auto &char_6 = char_1;
  auto char_7 = char_3;
  char char_8{'n'};
  auto &char_9 = char_2;
  auto char_10 = char_4;
  char_10 = 'w';
  char char_12{'i'};
  function(char_2, char_12);
  char char_13{'p'};
  char_9 = 'e';
  auto char_15 = char_4;
  auto &char_16 = char_15;
  char char_17{'v'};
  auto char_18 = char_10;
  auto &char_19 = char_2;
  char char_20{'s'};
  char_17 = 't';
  auto char_22 = char_3;
  char_15 = 'd';
  auto char_24 = char_22;
  function(char_2, char_16);
  char_4 = 'd';
  char char_26{'u'};
  print("{}{}{}{}{}{}{}",
```

```
        char_13, char_2, char_8, char_4, char_1, char_12,
        char_17);
}
```

// Answer (11):

// __ __ __ __ __ __ __ __ __ __ __
____

Solutions

Solution 1

```
void run() {
  char char_1{'q'};
  char_1 = 'c';
  char char_3{'h'};
  char_3 = 'y';
  char char_5{'p'};
  char_5 = 'l';
  char char_7{'t'};
  char_1 = 'f';
  char char_9{'r'};
  print("{}{}{}",                              // trl
        char_7, char_9, char_5);
}

// Answer: trl
```

Solution 2

```
void run() {
  char char_1{'h'};
  char_1 = 'm';
  char char_3{'q'};
  char_3 = 'o';
  char char_5{'h'};
  char_1 = 'r';
  char char_7{'v'};
  char_5 = 'i';
  char char_9{'s'};
  print("{}{}",                                // is
        char_5, char_9);
}

// Answer: is
```

Solution 3

```
void run() {
  char char_1{'m'};
  char_1 = 'p';
  char char_3{'o'};
  char_1 = 'x';
  char char_5{'S'};
  char_3 = 'n';
  char char_7{'R'};
  char_1 = 'h';
  char char_9{'X'};
  char_3 = 'A';
  char char_11{'k'};
  print("{}{}{}{}",                              // SARX
        char_5, char_3, char_7, char_9);
}

// Answer: SARX
```

Solution 4

```
void run() {
  char char_1{'a'};
  char_1 = 'b';
  char char_3{'u'};
  char_3 = 'c';
  char char_5{'u'};
  char_1 = 'n';
  char char_7{'o'};
  char_3 = 'v';
  char char_9{'t'};
  char_1 = 'r';
  char char_11{'b'};
  print("{}{}",                                  // or
        char_7, char_1);
}

// Answer: or
```

Solution 5

```
void run() {
  char char_1{'d'};
  char_1 = 'i';
  char char_3{'y'};
  char_3 = 'd';
  char char_5{'j'};
  char_3 = 'u';
  char char_7{'l'};
  char_5 = 'c';
  char char_9{'a'};
  char_9 = 'R';
  char char_11{'L'};
  char_1 = 'O';
  char char_13{'t'};
  print("{}{}{}",                          // ROL
        char_9, char_1, char_11);
}

// Answer: ROL
```

Solution 6

```
void run() {
  char char_1{'y'};
  char_1 = 'n';
  char char_3{'v'};
  char_3 = 'b';
  char char_5{'e'};
  char_1 = 'x';
  char char_7{'d'};
  char_5 = 'b';
  char char_9{'t'};
  char_3 = 'e';
  char char_11{'h'};
  char_5 = 'm';
  char char_13{'b'};
  print("{}{}",                            // tm
        char_9, char_5);
}

// Answer: tm
```

Solution 7

```
void run() {
  char char_1{'g'};
  char char_2{'o'};
  char_1 = 'r';
  char char_4{'q'};
  char_4 = 'n';
  char char_6{'q'};
  char_2 = 'f';
  char char_8{'x'};
  char_1 = 'r';
  char char_10{'e'};
  char_4 = 'n';
  char char_12{'g'};
  char_12 = 'u';
  char char_14{'w'};
  print("{}{}{}",                              // erf
        char_10, char_1, char_2);
}

// Answer: erf
```

Solution 8

```
void run() {
  char char_1{'j'};
  char_1 = 'c';
  char char_3{'m'};
  char_1 = 'g';
  char char_5{'g'};
  char_3 = 'd';
  char char_7{'w'};
  char_5 = 's';
  char char_9{'a'};
  char_7 = 't';
  char char_11{'b'};
  char_7 = 'e';
  char char_13{'c'};
  char_1 = 'c';
  char char_15{'b'};
  print("{}{}{}{}",                            // deca
        char_3, char_7, char_1, char_9);
```

```
}
```


Solution 9

```
void run() {
  char char_1{'s'};
  auto char_2 = char_1;
  char_2 = 'm';
  char char_4{'w'};
  char_2 = 'p';
  char char_6{'g'};
  auto char_7 = char_1;
  print("{}{}",                              // ws
        char_4, char_7);
}
```


Solution 10

```
void run() {
  char char_1{'f'};
  auto char_2 = char_1;
  char char_3{'d'};
  auto char_4 = char_1;
  char char_5{'i'};
  print("{}{}",                              // if
        char_5, char_4);
}
```

Solution 11

```
void run() {
  char char_1{'e'};
  char_1 = 'y';
  char char_3{'r'};
  auto char_4 = char_3;
  char_3 = 'e';
  auto char_6 = char_3;
  char char_7{'a'};
  char_1 = 'f';
  char char_9{'t'};
  print("{}{}{}{}",                              // tera
        char_9, char_6, char_4, char_7);
}

// Answer: tera
```

Solution 12

```
void run() {
  char char_1{'v'};
  auto char_2 = char_1;
  char_1 = 'h';
  auto char_4 = char_2;
  char_2 = 'u';
  auto char_6 = char_4;
  char_2 = 'R';
  char char_8{'O'};
  auto char_9 = char_2;
  print("{}{}{}",                                // ROR
        char_2, char_8, char_9);
}

// Answer: ROR
```

Solution 13

```
void run() {
  char char_1{'d'};
  auto char_2 = char_1;
  char_2 = 'q';
  char char_4{'e'};
  char_2 = 'n';
  char char_6{'a'};
  auto char_7 = char_6;
  char char_8{'m'};
  char_1 = 'x';
  auto char_10 = char_7;
  print("{}{}{}",                         // exa
        char_4, char_1, char_7);
}

// Answer: exa
```

Solution 14

```
void run() {
  char char_1{'d'};
  char char_2{'n'};
  char_1 = 'b';
  auto char_4 = char_2;
  char_1 = 'd';
  auto char_6 = char_1;
  char char_7{'f'};
  auto char_8 = char_6;
  char_7 = 'a';
  auto char_10 = char_2;
  print("{}{}{}",                         // nan
        char_2, char_7, char_10);
}

// Answer: nan
```

Solution 15

```cpp
void run() {
  char char_1{'v'};
  auto char_2 = char_1;
  char char_3{'p'};
  auto char_4 = char_3;
  char char_5{'v'};
  char_4 = 'w';
  char char_7{'k'};
  char_1 = 'o';
  char char_9{'w'};
  char_4 = 'f';
  auto char_11 = char_9;
  print("{}{}{}",                              // pow
        char_3, char_1, char_9);
}

// Answer: pow
```

Solution 16

```cpp
void run() {
  char char_1{'r'};
  char_1 = 'm';
  char char_3{'i'};
  auto char_4 = char_1;
  char_4 = 'M';
  char char_6{'v'};
  char_1 = 'u';
  auto char_8 = char_3;
  char_3 = 'e';
  auto char_10 = char_3;
  char char_11{'o'};
  auto char_12 = char_11;
  print("{}{}{}{}",                            // Move
        char_4, char_11, char_6, char_3);
}

// Answer: Move
```

Solution 17

```
void run() {
  char char_1{'i'};
  auto &char_2 = char_1;
  char_2 = 'g';
  auto &char_4 = char_1;
  char_4 = 'd';
  char char_6{'o'};
  auto &char_7 = char_6;
  print("{}{}",                              // do
        char_1, char_7);
}

// Answer: do
```

Solution 18

```
void run() {
  char char_1{'e'};
  char_1 = 'v';
  char char_3{'c'};
  char_1 = 'm';
  char char_5{'p'};
  auto &char_6 = char_5;
  char_5 = 'n';
  char char_8{'i'};
  print("{}{}{}",                            // min
        char_1, char_8, char_6);
}

// Answer: min
```

Solution 19

```
void run() {
  char char_1{'s'};
  auto &char_2 = char_1;
  char_1 = 'd';
  auto &char_4 = char_1;
  char char_5{'k'};
  char_5 = 'C';
  char char_7{'q'};
```

```cpp
  char_2 = 'R';
  auto &char_9 = char_1;
  print("{}{}{}",                                         // RCR
        char_1, char_5, char_4);
}

// Answer: RCR
```

Solution 20

```cpp
void run() {
  char char_1{'d'};
  auto &char_2 = char_1;
  char char_3{'n'};
  char_2 = 'c';
  char char_5{'F'};
  char_2 = 'q';
  auto &char_7 = char_1;
  char_1 = 'L';
  char char_9{'S'};
  print("{}{}{}",                                         // LFS
        char_7, char_5, char_9);
}

// Answer: LFS
```

Solution 21

```cpp
void run() {
  char char_1{'i'};
  auto &char_2 = char_1;
  char_1 = 'p';
  auto &char_4 = char_2;
  char_1 = 'l';
  char char_6{'L'};
  auto &char_7 = char_2;
  char char_8{'y'};
  char_1 = 'S';
  auto &char_10 = char_4;
  print("{}{}{}",                                         // LSS
        char_6, char_1, char_2);
}
```

```
// Answer: LSS
```

Solution 22

```
void run() {
  char char_1{'s'};
  auto &char_2 = char_1;
  char_2 = 'w';
  char char_4{'i'};
  char_2 = 'S';
  char char_6{'g'};
  auto &char_7 = char_2;
  char_4 = 'C';
  char char_9{'A'};
  char_6 = 's';
  auto &char_11 = char_2;
  print("{}{}{}{}",                        // SCAS
        char_7, char_4, char_9, char_1);
}
```

```
// Answer: SCAS
```

Solution 23

```
void run() {
  char char_1{'w'};
  auto &char_2 = char_1;
  char_2 = 'r';
  auto &char_4 = char_1;
  char char_5{'w'};
  char_4 = 'e';
  char char_7{'R'};
  auto &char_8 = char_1;
  char_5 = 'P';
  char char_10{'o'};
  char_2 = 'E';
  auto &char_12 = char_8;
  print("{}{}{}{}",                        // REPE
        char_7, char_1, char_5, char_2);
}
```

```
// Answer: REPE
```

Solution 24

```cpp
void run() {
  char char_1{'w'};
  auto &char_2 = char_1;
  char_2 = 'a';
  auto &char_4 = char_2;
  char char_5{'k'};
  auto &char_6 = char_4;
  char_6 = 'q';
  char char_8{'m'};
  char_4 = 'v';
  char char_10{'a'};
  char_2 = 's';
  char char_12{'m'};
  print("{}{}{}",                         // asm
        char_10, char_1, char_8);
}


// Answer: asm
```

Solution 25

```cpp
void run() {
  char char_1{'a'};
  char_1 = 'r';
  print("{}",                             // r
        char_1);
  char char_3{'q'};
  auto char_4 = char_3;
  char char_5{'s'};
  char_3 = 'i';
  char char_7{'u'};
  auto char_8 = char_1;
  char char_9{'e'};
  auto &char_10 = char_7;
  print("{}{}{}",                         // equ
        char_9, char_4, char_7);
  auto char_11 = char_1;
  char char_12{'e'};
  print("{}{}{}{}",                       // ires
        char_3, char_11, char_12, char_5);
}
```

```cpp
// Answer: requires
```

Solution 26

```cpp
void run() {
  char char_1{'u'};
  char_1 = 't';
  auto char_3 = char_1;
  char_1 = 'r';
  char char_5{'o'};
  auto char_6 = char_1;
  auto &char_7 = char_3;
  char char_8{'l'};
  char_1 = 's';
  print("{}{}{}",                        // str
        char_1, char_7, char_6);
  auto &char_10 = char_5;
  char char_11{'d'};
  char_5 = 'p';
  char char_13{'o'};
  auto char_14 = char_10;
  print("{}{}{}",                        // tod
        char_3, char_13, char_11);
}
```

```cpp
// Answer: strtod
```

Solution 27

```cpp
void run() {
  char char_1{'S'};
  auto &char_2 = char_1;
  auto char_3 = char_1;
  char_2 = 'v';
  auto &char_5 = char_1;
  char_5 = 'D';
  auto char_7 = char_2;
  char_7 = 'r';
  auto &char_9 = char_3;
  char char_10{'w'};
  auto char_11 = char_1;
  char_11 = 'y';
```

```
  auto char_13 = char_7;
  char char_14{'L'};
  print("{}{}{}",                                        // LDS
        char_14, char_1, char_3);
}

// Answer: LDS
```

Solution 28

```
void run() {
  char char_1{'T'};
  auto char_2 = char_1;
  auto &char_3 = char_2;
  auto char_4 = char_1;
  char_3 = 'c';
  char char_6{'q'};
  char_3 = 'S';
  auto char_8 = char_3;
  char char_9{'x'};
  char_6 = 'k';
  auto char_11 = char_2;
  char char_12{'O'};
  auto char_13 = char_6;
  print("{}{}{}{}",                                      // STOS
        char_11, char_1, char_12, char_3);
}

// Answer: STOS
```

Solution 29

```
void run() {
  char char_1{'t'};
  char_1 = 's';
  print("{}",                                            // s
        char_1);
  auto char_3 = char_1;
  char_1 = 'j';
  char char_5{'d'};
  auto char_6 = char_1;
  char_6 = 'q';
  auto &char_8 = char_1;
```

```cpp
    auto char_9 = char_5;
    auto &char_10 = char_9;
    char char_11{'b'};
    auto &char_12 = char_10;
    char_1 = 'e';
    auto &char_14 = char_1;
    auto char_15 = char_12;
    print("{}{}{}",                          // eed
          char_14, char_8, char_12);
}

// Answer: seed
```

Solution 30

```cpp
void run() {
  char char_1{'S'};
  auto &char_2 = char_1;
  char char_3{'F'};
  print("{}{}",                              // FS
        char_3, char_2);
  char_2 = 'B';
  char char_5{'x'};
  char_5 = 'U';
  auto char_7 = char_1;
  char_3 = 'R';
  char char_9{'s'};
  auto char_10 = char_3;
  auto &char_11 = char_9;
  char_9 = 'P';
  auto &char_13 = char_9;
  char char_14{'l'};
  auto char_15 = char_10;
  print("{}{}{}{}",                          // UBRP
        char_5, char_7, char_15, char_13);
}

// Answer: FSUBRP
```

Solution 31

```cpp
void run() {
  char char_1{'u'};
  char char_2{'b'};
  char_1 = 'i';
  char char_4{'n'};
  char_2 = 's';
  auto &char_6 = char_4;
  char_4 = 't';
  char char_8{'m'};
  char_8 = 'o';
  char char_10{'c'};
  auto char_11 = char_2;
  char_4 = 'r';
  auto char_13 = char_8;
  char_2 = 'j';
  char char_15{'_'};
  auto &char_16 = char_4;
  char_2 = 'm';
  char char_18{'e'};
  print("{}{}{}{}{}{}{}",                          // io_errc
        char_1, char_13, char_15, char_18, char_16, char_6,
        char_10);
}

// Answer: io_errc
```

Solution 32

```cpp
void run() {
  char char_1{'o'};
  char char_2{'l'};
  auto char_3 = char_2;
  auto &char_4 = char_2;
  char_3 = 'd';
  auto &char_6 = char_1;
  auto char_7 = char_3;
  char char_8{'w'};
  char_8 = 'w';
  auto &char_10 = char_7;
  char_8 = 'p';
  auto &char_12 = char_2;
```

```cpp
  char char_13{'A'};
  auto char_14 = char_8;
  print("{}{}{}",                              // Add
        char_13, char_3, char_7);
}
```

```
// Answer: Add
```

Solution 33

```cpp
void run() {
  char char_1{'q'};
  char_1 = '.';
  auto char_3 = char_1;
  char_1 = 'c';
  print("{}",                                  // c
        char_1);
  auto &char_5 = char_3;
  auto char_6 = char_1;
  char_6 = 'f';
  auto char_8 = char_1;
  auto &char_9 = char_5;
  char_6 = 'p';
  char char_11{'p'};
  auto &char_12 = char_6;
  char char_13{'l'};
  char_1 = 'w';
  char char_15{'s'};
  print("{}{}{}{}",                            // pp.s
        char_12, char_6, char_9, char_15);
  char_3 = 'e';
  char char_17{'o'};
  print("{}{}{}{}",                            // cope
        char_8, char_17, char_11, char_3);
}
```

```
// Answer: cpp.scope
```

Solution 34

```
void run() {
  char char_1{'P'};
  auto &char_2 = char_1;
  print("{}",                                      // P
        char_1);
  auto char_3 = char_2;
  char char_4{'H'};
  print("{}",                                      // H
        char_4);
  char_1 = 'D';
  auto &char_6 = char_1;
  auto char_7 = char_2;
  char_7 = 'd';
  char char_9{'u'};
  auto char_10 = char_1;
  char char_11{'f'};
  char_3 = 'A';
  char char_13{'b'};
  auto char_14 = char_2;
  print("{}{}{}{}",                                // ADDD
        char_3, char_6, char_2, char_14);
}

// Answer: PHADDD
```

Solution 35

```
void run() {
  char char_1{'k'};
  char_1 = 'e';
  auto &char_3 = char_1;
  char char_4{'n'};
  char_3 = 'a';
  auto &char_6 = char_4;
  char char_7{'t'};
  char_7 = 'a';
  char char_9{'g'};
  auto char_10 = char_7;
  char char_11{'o'};
  char_9 = 'q';
  auto char_13 = char_3;
```

```cpp
  char_10 = 'o';
  auto char_15 = char_3;
  char char_16{'a'};
  print("{}{}{}{}",                                  // nano
        char_4, char_3, char_6, char_11);
}

// Answer: nano
```

Solution 36

```cpp
void run() {
  char char_1{'d'};
  auto char_2 = char_1;
  char_2 = 'w';
  auto char_4 = char_1;
  auto &char_5 = char_1;
  char_2 = 'e';
  auto &char_7 = char_4;
  char_4 = 'n';
  char char_9{'h'};
  auto char_10 = char_1;
  char_10 = 'e';
  auto char_12 = char_4;
  auto &char_13 = char_5;
  char_12 = 'p';
  auto &char_15 = char_13;
  auto char_16 = char_1;
  print("{}{}{}",                                    // end
        char_10, char_4, char_5);
}

// Answer: end
```

Solution 37

```cpp
void run() {
  char char_1{'f'};
  char_1 = 'r';
  char char_3{'c'};
  char_3 = 'w';
  auto &char_5 = char_3;
  auto char_6 = char_5;
  print("{}",                                      // w
        char_6);
  char_3 = 'h';
  auto &char_8 = char_6;
  char char_9{'c'};
  char_6 = 'o';
  char char_11{'m'};
  auto &char_12 = char_11;
  char char_13{'b'};
  char_3 = 'f';
  auto &char_15 = char_12;
  auto char_16 = char_3;
  char_6 = 't';
  char char_18{'o'};
  print("{}{}{}{}{}{}",                            // crtomb
        char_9, char_1, char_8, char_18, char_11, char_13);
}

// Answer: wcrtomb
```

Solution 38

```cpp
void run() {
  char char_1{'r'};
  char_1 = 't';
  print("{}",                                      // t
        char_1);
  auto char_3 = char_1;
  char_1 = 'm';
  auto char_5 = char_3;
  char char_6{'f'};
  auto char_7 = char_6;
  char_6 = 'g';
  char char_9{'a'};
```

```cpp
  auto &char_10 = char_3;
  char char_11{'q'};
  char_5 = 'k';
  char char_13{'m'};
  auto &char_14 = char_6;
  char char_15{'a'};
  auto char_16 = char_1;
  print("{}{}{}{}{}{}",                          // gammaf
        char_14, char_15, char_16, char_13, char_9, char_7);
}

// Answer: tgammaf
```

Solution 39

```cpp
void run() {
  char char_1{'j'};
  char_1 = 'm';
  auto char_3 = char_1;
  print("{}",                                    // m
        char_3);
  char_3 = 'g';
  char char_5{'r'};
  auto &char_6 = char_3;
  char_6 = 'e';
  char char_8{'w'};
  char_5 = 'q';
  auto char_10 = char_1;
  char char_11{'o'};
  char_10 = 'd';
  char char_13{'k'};
  auto &char_14 = char_10;
  auto char_15 = char_3;
  char_5 = 'v';
  char char_17{'m'};
  auto &char_18 = char_6;
  print("{}{}{}{}{}{}",                          // emmove
        char_15, char_17, char_1, char_11, char_5, char_6);
}

// Answer: memmove
```

Solution 40

```cpp
void run() {
  char char_1{'b'};
  char_1 = 'm';
  auto &char_3 = char_1;
  char char_4{'t'};
  char_1 = 'h';
  auto char_6 = char_4;
  char char_7{'g'};
  char_1 = 'o';
  auto &char_9 = char_4;
  char char_10{'n'};
  auto &char_11 = char_7;
  char char_12{'b'};
  auto char_13 = char_11;
  char char_14{'i'};
  char_9 = 'l';
  char char_16{'l'};
  print("{}{}{}{}{}{}",                              // ilogbl
        char_14, char_9, char_1, char_13, char_12, char_16);
}


// Answer: ilogbl
```

Solution 41

```cpp
void run() {
  char char_1{'L'};
  auto char_2 = char_1;
  char char_3{'o'};
  auto char_4 = char_1;
  char char_5{'b'};
  char_1 = 'D';
  char char_7{'2'};
  char_5 = 'E';
  auto char_9 = char_1;
  char char_10{'s'};
  char_9 = 'x';
  auto &char_12 = char_7;
  auto char_13 = char_9;
  auto &char_14 = char_4;
  char char_15{'F'};
```

```
  print("{}{}{}{}{}{}",                                    // FLDL2E
        char_15, char_14, char_1, char_4, char_12, char_5);
}

// Answer: FLDL2E
```

Solution 42

```
void run() {
  char char_1{'r'};
  auto char_2 = char_1;
  auto &char_3 = char_1;
  auto char_4 = char_1;
  char char_5{'s'};
  char_4 = 'r';
  auto char_7 = char_2;
  char_2 = 'm';
  auto char_9 = char_7;
  char_2 = 'o';
  char char_11{'r'};
  char_9 = 'd';
  auto char_13 = char_5;
  char char_14{'t'};
  auto &char_15 = char_5;
  char char_16{'e'};
  print("{}{}{}{}{}{}{}{}",                            // strerror
        char_13, char_14, char_4, char_16, char_3, char_1,
        char_2, char_11);
}

// Answer: strerror
```

Solution 43

```
void run() {
  char char_1{'n'};
  auto char_2 = char_1;
  char char_3{'s'};
  char_2 = 's';
  print("{}",                                    // s
        char_2);
  char char_5{'p'};
  auto &char_6 = char_1;
```

```cpp
  char_6 = ':';
  print("{}",                                    // p
        char_5);
  char char_8{'i'};
  char_2 = 'n';
  auto &char_10 = char_2;
  char char_11{'a'};
  print("{}{}{}{}",                              // an::
        char_11, char_10, char_6, char_1);
  auto &char_12 = char_3;
  print("{}",                                    // s
        char_3);
  char_12 = 'z';
  print("{}",                                    // i
        char_8);
  char char_14{'e'};
  print("{}",                                    // z
        char_12);
  char char_15{'x'};
  auto &char_16 = char_12;
  print("{}",                                    // e
        char_14);
}

// Answer: span::size
```

Solution 44

```cpp
void run() {
  char char_1{'o'};
  char_1 = 'l';
  auto &char_3 = char_1;
  char char_4{'d'};
  auto char_5 = char_4;
  char_1 = 'k';
  char char_7{'g'};
  char_5 = 'n';
  print("{}",                                    // n
        char_5);
  char char_9{'p'};
  auto &char_10 = char_3;
  auto char_11 = char_10;
  auto &char_12 = char_5;
```

```
    char char_13{'k'};
    auto char_14 = char_7;
    char_3 = 'o';
    auto char_16 = char_12;
    print("{}{}{}",                              // oop
          char_1, char_10, char_9);
}

// Answer: noop
```

Solution 45

```
void run() {
    char char_1{'w'};
    char_1 = 'o';
    char char_3{'i'};
    auto &char_4 = char_1;
    char char_5{'e'};
    auto char_6 = char_3;
    char_5 = 'y';
    char char_8{'a'};
    char_1 = 'p';
    auto char_10 = char_4;
    char_6 = 'o';
    auto &char_12 = char_8;
    char_8 = 'e';
    char char_14{'r'};
    auto &char_15 = char_6;
    char char_16{'k'};
    auto char_17 = char_6;
    char_15 = 'l';
    char char_19{'t'};
    print("{}{}{}{}",                            // lerp
          char_15, char_8, char_14, char_4);
}

// Answer: lerp
```

Solution 46

```
void run() {
  char char_1{'u'};
  char_1 = 'l';
  auto &char_3 = char_1;
  print("{}",                                    // l
        char_3);
  char_1 = 'j';
  char char_5{'x'};
  auto &char_6 = char_1;
  char char_7{'j'};
  auto &char_8 = char_5;
  char char_9{'v'};
  auto &char_10 = char_6;
  char_10 = 'd';
  auto char_12 = char_5;
  char_5 = '_';
  auto char_14 = char_3;
  char char_15{'i'};
  auto char_16 = char_14;
  char char_17{'t'};
  print("{}{}{}{}{}",                            // div_t
        char_16, char_15, char_9, char_8, char_17);
}


// Answer: ldiv_t
```

Solution 47

```
void run() {
  char char_1{'q'};
  char char_2{'c'};
  char_1 = '.';
  char char_4{'n'};
  print("{}",                                    // c
        char_2);
  char_2 = 'y';
  auto char_6 = char_1;
  char_6 = 'p';
  auto char_8 = char_4;
  auto &char_9 = char_2;
  char_8 = 'x';
```

```cpp
  auto char_11 = char_2;
  char_11 = 'q';
  char char_13{'n'};
  auto &char_14 = char_9;
  char char_15{'p'};
  char_13 = 'u';
  auto char_17 = char_13;
  char char_18{'a'};
  print("{}{}{}{}{}",                          // pp.nu
        char_15, char_6, char_1, char_4, char_17);
  char_2 = 'l';
  char char_20{'c'};
  print("{}{}",                                // ll
        char_14, char_9);
}


// Answer: cpp.null
```

Solution 48

```cpp
void run() {
  char char_1{'i'};
  auto &char_2 = char_1;
  char_2 = 'g';
  print("{}",                                  // g
        char_2);
  char_1 = 'e';
  print("{}",                                  // e
        char_1);
  char_2 = 'n';
  auto char_6 = char_2;
  char char_7{'a'};
  print("{}",                                  // n
        char_6);
  char_2 = 'e';
  auto char_9 = char_2;
  auto &char_10 = char_7;
  auto char_11 = char_9;
  char_1 = 'i';
  auto &char_13 = char_6;
  char_1 = 'y';
  auto &char_15 = char_13;
  char char_16{'t'};
```

```cpp
  auto char_17 = char_2;
  char_2 = 'u';
  char char_19{'r'};
  auto char_20 = char_11;
  print("{}{}{}{}{}",                              // erate
        char_20, char_19, char_7, char_16, char_11);
}

// Answer: generate
```

Solution 49

```cpp
void run() {
  char char_1{'v'};
  char_1 = 'r';
  auto char_3 = char_1;
  auto &char_4 = char_1;
  auto char_5 = char_3;
  char char_6{'p'};
  auto &char_7 = char_3;
  char char_8{'g'};
  auto char_9 = char_3;
  auto &char_10 = char_6;
  char_10 = 't';
  auto &char_12 = char_8;
  char_3 = 's';
  auto char_14 = char_10;
  char_1 = 'k';
  auto char_16 = char_9;
  char char_17{'s'};
  print("{}{}{}{}{}{}",                            // strstr
        char_17, char_14, char_9, char_7, char_6, char_16);
}

// Answer: strstr
```

Solution 50

```cpp
void run() {
  char char_1{'l'};
  auto &char_2 = char_1;
  char char_3{'v'};
  auto &char_4 = char_1;
  auto char_5 = char_2;
  print("{}{}",                          // ll
        char_4, char_5);
  auto &char_6 = char_3;
  auto char_7 = char_1;
  auto &char_8 = char_3;
  char char_9{'q'};
  char_3 = 's';
  auto &char_11 = char_9;
  char_11 = 'a';
  auto char_13 = char_2;
  char_5 = 'g';
  char char_15{'b'};
  auto char_16 = char_9;
  print("{}{}{}",                        // abs
        char_16, char_15, char_3);
}

// Answer: llabs
```

Solution 51

```cpp
void run() {
  char char_1{'n'};
  char_1 = 'i';
  char char_3{'t'};
  auto char_4 = char_3;
  auto &char_5 = char_1;
  auto char_6 = char_1;
  char_1 = 'n';
  print("{}{}",                          // in
        char_6, char_1);
  char char_8{'t'};
  char_1 = '8';
  auto &char_10 = char_6;
  char_6 = 'd';
```

```cpp
  auto char_12 = char_5;
  char char_13{'q'};
  auto &char_14 = char_8;
  char char_15{'c'};
  auto char_16 = char_3;
  char_8 = '_';
  auto char_18 = char_10;
  print("{}{}{}{}",                                    // t8_t
        char_4, char_5, char_14, char_16);
}
```

```cpp
// Answer: int8_t
```

Solution 52

```cpp
void run() {
  char char_1{'a'};
  char_1 = 'r';
  auto char_3 = char_1;
  char_3 = 'p';
  char char_5{'t'};
  auto char_6 = char_3;
  auto &char_7 = char_3;
  char_1 = 'm';
  auto char_9 = char_1;
  char char_10{'y'};
  auto &char_11 = char_3;
  char_10 = 'y';
  char char_13{'d'};
  char_7 = 'a';
  auto char_15 = char_9;
  auto &char_16 = char_3;
  char char_17{'g'};
  auto char_18 = char_17;
  print("{}{}{}{}{}{}",                                // tgamma
        char_5, char_18, char_3, char_15, char_9, char_11);
}
```

```cpp
// Answer: tgamma
```

Solution 53

```cpp
void run() {
  char char_1{'q'};
  auto char_2 = char_1;
  char char_3{'y'};
  char_2 = 'm';
  char char_5{'o'};
  auto &char_6 = char_1;
  char_3 = '_';
  char char_8{'g'};
  auto char_9 = char_2;
  char_1 = 'x';
  char char_11{'f'};
  auto &char_12 = char_8;
  char char_13{'a'};
  auto char_14 = char_8;
  char_14 = 'l';
  char char_16{'v'};
  auto &char_17 = char_9;
  char_1 = 'l';
  auto &char_19 = char_12;
  print("{}{}{}{}{}{}",                          // all_of
        char_13, char_6, char_1, char_3, char_5, char_11);
}


// Answer: all_of
```

Solution 54

```cpp
void run() {
  char char_1{'s'};
  auto char_2 = char_1;
  char char_3{'h'};
  auto char_4 = char_1;
  char char_5{'d'};
  char_3 = 'e';
  char char_7{'a'};
  auto &char_8 = char_3;
  char char_9{'g'};
  char_1 = 's';
  auto &char_11 = char_1;
  auto char_12 = char_4;
```

```cpp
  char char_13{'b'};
  auto char_14 = char_13;
  char char_15{'m'};
  auto &char_16 = char_7;
  print("{}{}{}{}{}{}{}{}",                          // messages
        char_15, char_3, char_12, char_1, char_7, char_9,
        char_8, char_11);
}
```

```
// Answer: messages
```

Solution 55

```cpp
void run() {
  char char_1{'x'};
  auto &char_2 = char_1;
  char_1 = 'u';
  auto &char_4 = char_1;
  char_2 = 'g';
  print("{}",                                        // g
        char_4);
  char_1 = 'r';
  print("{}",                                        // r
        char_2);
  char_2 = 'l';
  auto char_8 = char_1;
  char char_9{'a'};
  auto &char_10 = char_2;
  char char_11{'u'};
  char_11 = '.';
  char char_13{'m'};
  auto &char_14 = char_10;
  char_10 = 'g';
  char char_16{'p'};
  char_1 = 'c';
  auto char_18 = char_4;
  char char_19{'d'};
  auto char_20 = char_14;
  auto &char_21 = char_11;
  print("{}{}{}{}{}{}",                              // am.dcl
        char_9, char_13, char_11, char_19, char_10, char_8);
}
```

```
// Answer: gram.dcl
```

Solution 56

```
void run() {
  char char_1{'e'};
  auto char_2 = char_1;
  char_1 = 'r';
  auto &char_4 = char_1;
  char char_5{'t'};
  print("{}{}",                                       // re
        char_4, char_2);
  auto &char_6 = char_1;
  char char_7{'h'};
  char_5 = 'a';
  char char_9{'t'};
  auto &char_10 = char_6;
  char char_11{'e'};
  auto &char_12 = char_9;
  char char_13{'u'};
  char_12 = 'l';
  char char_15{'w'};
  auto char_16 = char_12;
  char_11 = 'g';
  auto char_18 = char_10;
  print("{}{}{}{}{}",                                 // gular
        char_11, char_13, char_12, char_5, char_10);
}
```

```
// Answer: regular
```

Solution 57

```
void run() {
  char char_1{'w'};
  auto &char_2 = char_1;
  char char_3{'d'};
  auto &char_4 = char_1;
  print("{}",                                         // w
        char_2);
  auto &char_5 = char_3;
  char char_6{'b'};
```

```cpp
  auto &char_7 = char_1;
  char_6 = 't';
  char char_9{'d'};
  auto &char_10 = char_1;
  char_6 = 'w';
  auto &char_12 = char_1;
  char_4 = 'c';
  auto &char_14 = char_4;
  char_3 = 'p';
  char char_16{'w'};
  char_9 = 's';
  auto &char_18 = char_9;
  char char_19{'n'};
  print("{}{}{}{}{}{}",                              // cscspn
        char_1, char_18, char_14, char_9, char_3, char_19);
}


// Answer: wcscspn
```

Solution 58

```cpp
void run() {
  char char_1{'k'};
  auto &char_2 = char_1;
  auto char_3 = char_1;
  char char_4{'P'};
  char_2 = 's';
  auto char_6 = char_4;
  auto &char_7 = char_4;
  char_2 = 'c';
  auto char_9 = char_3;
  char_4 = 'm';
  char char_11{'O'};
  auto &char_12 = char_1;
  char char_13{'L'};
  auto &char_14 = char_4;
  char char_15{'j'};
  char_7 = 'u';
  auto char_17 = char_6;
  char_15 = 'O';
  auto char_19 = char_14;
  print("{}{}{}{}{}{}",                          // LOOPcc
        char_13, char_15, char_11, char_17, char_1, char_2);
```

```
}
```


Solution 59

```
void run() {
  char char_1{'t'};
  char char_2{'e'};
  auto &char_3 = char_2;
  char char_4{'d'};
  auto &char_5 = char_4;
  auto char_6 = char_3;
  print("{}{}",                              // de
        char_4, char_3);
  auto char_7 = char_1;
  auto &char_8 = char_7;
  auto char_9 = char_6;
  char char_10{'l'};
  auto &char_11 = char_4;
  char_8 = 'e';
  auto &char_13 = char_8;
  auto char_14 = char_1;
  char char_15{'t'};
  print("{}{}{}{}",                          // lete
        char_10, char_6, char_14, char_13);
}
```


Solution 60

```
void run() {
  char char_1{'u'};
  auto &char_2 = char_1;
  char_2 = 'O';
  auto &char_4 = char_2;
  char char_5{'b'};
  auto &char_6 = char_5;
  char_5 = 'F';
  auto char_8 = char_6;
  char_5 = 'P';
  char char_10{'Q'};
```

```cpp
  auto char_11 = char_4;
  auto &char_12 = char_8;
  auto char_13 = char_10;
  auto &char_14 = char_6;
  auto char_15 = char_6;
  auto &char_16 = char_10;
  auto char_17 = char_1;
  print("{}{}{}{}{}",                              // POPFQ
        char_6, char_2, char_5, char_12, char_13);
}
```

// Answer: POPFQ

Solution 61

```cpp
void run() {
  char char_1{'q'};
  auto char_2 = char_1;
  auto &char_3 = char_2;
  char char_4{'a'};
  char_3 = 'r';
  auto char_6 = char_4;
  auto &char_7 = char_1;
  char char_8{'y'};
  auto &char_9 = char_3;
  auto char_10 = char_2;
  char_7 = 'p';
  char char_12{'g'};
  auto &char_13 = char_9;
  auto char_14 = char_3;
  char_7 = 'n';
  auto char_16 = char_8;
  char char_17{'a'};
  auto &char_18 = char_2;
  print("{}{}{}{}{}",                           // array
        char_17, char_9, char_13, char_4, char_16);
}
```

// Answer: array

Solution 62

```cpp
void run() {
  char char_1{'r'};
  print("{}",                             // r
        char_1);
  char char_2{'f'};
  auto char_3 = char_2;
  char char_4{'.'};
  char_2 = 'e';
  print("{}{}",                           // e.
        char_2, char_4);
  char char_6{'n'};
  auto &char_7 = char_2;
  auto char_8 = char_1;
  char_1 = 'c';
  auto char_10 = char_2;
  char_3 = 'r';
  char char_12{'x'};
  char_8 = 'i';
  char char_14{'x'};
  auto &char_15 = char_1;
  char_10 = 'r';
  char char_17{'e'};
  auto char_18 = char_1;
  char_8 = 'f';
  auto &char_20 = char_6;
  char_20 = 'g';
  auto &char_22 = char_20;
  print("{}{}{}{}{}",                     // regex
        char_10, char_7, char_6, char_17, char_14);
}

// Answer: re.regex
```

Solution 63

```cpp
void run() {
  char char_1{'s'};
  auto char_2 = char_1;
  print("{}",                                    // s
        char_1);
  auto char_3 = char_2;
  auto &char_4 = char_2;
  char_2 = 'l';
  char char_6{'f'};
  auto char_7 = char_6;
  char char_8{'n'};
  char_8 = 't';
  char char_10{'v'};
  auto &char_11 = char_3;
  auto char_12 = char_3;
  char_10 = '_';
  auto &char_14 = char_10;
  char char_15{'l'};
  char_7 = 'z';
  char char_17{'m'};
  char_17 = 'i';
  auto char_19 = char_3;
  char char_20{'e'};
  print("{}{}{}{}{}",                            // ize_t
        char_17, char_7, char_20, char_14, char_8);
}

// Answer: size_t
```

Solution 64

```cpp
void run() {
  char char_1{'y'};
  char_1 = 'r';
  char char_3{'f'};
  char_3 = 'c';
  char char_5{'v'};
  auto &char_6 = char_3;
  char_6 = 'e';
  auto &char_8 = char_3;
  char char_9{'s'};
```

```cpp
    auto char_10 = char_9;
    char char_11{'v'};
    auto char_12 = char_8;
    char char_13{'h'};
    char_5 = 'k';
    auto char_15 = char_13;
    char_5 = 'j';
    auto &char_17 = char_13;
    char_13 = 'r';
    auto char_19 = char_1;
    char_19 = 'r';
    char char_21{'e'};
    char_5 = 'y';
    auto &char_23 = char_11;
    print("{}{}{}{}{}{}{}",                          // reverse
          char_17, char_21, char_23, char_6, char_1, char_9,
          char_3);
}

// Answer: reverse
```

Solution 65

```cpp
auto function(char &parameter_1, char parameter_2) {
  parameter_1 = 't';
  char char_2{':'};
  parameter_1 = 'd';
  auto char_4 = char_2;
  print("{}{}",
        parameter_1, parameter_2);
  char char_5{'i'};
  print("{}{}",
        char_2, char_5);
}
void run() {
  char char_1{'t'};
  auto char_2 = char_1;
  char_1 = 'd';
  print("{}",                                        // t
        char_2);
  char char_4{'a'};
  char_1 = 'i';
  auto char_6 = char_2;
```

```
  char char_7{'r'};
  auto char_8 = char_6;
  char_8 = ':';
  auto char_10 = char_4;
  char_1 = 'w';
  char char_12{'h'};
  char_1 = 'e';
  char char_14{'d'};
  auto &char_15 = char_14;
  print("{}{}{}{}",                               // hrea
        char_12, char_7, char_1, char_10);
  function(char_10, char_8);                       // d:
                                                   // :i

  print("{}",                                      // d
        char_14);
}


// Answer: thread::id
```

Solution 66

```
auto function(char &parameter_1, char &parameter_2) {
  char char_1{'a'};
  auto char_2 = char_1;
  print("{}",
        parameter_1);
  auto char_3 = parameter_1;
  char char_4{'g'};
  print("{}{}",
        char_4, char_1);
}
void run() {
  char char_1{'a'};
  char char_2{'m'};
  auto char_3 = char_2;
  auto &char_4 = char_2;
  char char_5{'l'};
  auto &char_6 = char_2;
  char char_7{'l'};
  auto char_8 = char_7;
  function(char_5, char_6);                        // l
                                                   // ga

  auto &char_9 = char_4;
```

```
  auto char_10 = char_1;
  print("{}{}{}{}",                          // mmal
        char_9, char_3, char_10, char_8);
}
```

```
// Answer: lgammal
```

Solution 67

```
auto function(char &parameter_1, char parameter_2) {
  parameter_2 = 'f';
  char char_2{'i'};
  auto &char_3 = parameter_1;
  char char_4{'l'};
  auto char_5 = parameter_1;
  parameter_2 = 'x';
  print("{}{}{}",
        char_2, char_3, parameter_1);
}
void run() {
  char char_1{'f'};
  auto char_2 = char_1;
  char char_3{'d'};
  auto char_4 = char_3;
  print("{}",                                // d
        char_4);
  char char_5{'v'};
  auto &char_6 = char_2;
  auto char_7 = char_3;
  function(char_6, char_3);                   // iff
  char_2 = '.';
  auto char_9 = char_5;
  char_5 = 'p';
  char char_11{'c'};
  char_1 = 'p';
  char char_13{'r'};
  char_13 = 'b';
  auto &char_15 = char_7;
  print("{}{}{}{}",                           // .cpp
        char_2, char_11, char_5, char_1);
}
```

```
// Answer: diff.cpp
```

Solution 68

```
auto function(char &parameter_1, char parameter_2) {
  parameter_1 = 'b';
  char char_2{'p'};
  parameter_1 = 'i';
  auto char_4 = parameter_1;
  auto &char_5 = parameter_2;
  char char_6{'o'};
  print("{}{}{}",
        char_2, char_6, char_4);
}
void run() {
  char char_1{'q'};
  char char_2{'p'};
  char_1 = 'i';
  auto &char_4 = char_2;
  char char_5{'s'};
  char_5 = 'o';
  function(char_2, char_1);                        // .poi
  auto &char_7 = char_5;
  char char_8{'s'};
  auto &char_9 = char_5;
  auto char_10 = char_8;
  char char_11{'n'};
  auto &char_12 = char_4;
  auto char_13 = char_11;
  print("{}{}{}{}",                                // sson
        char_10, char_8, char_5, char_13);
}

// Answer: poisson
```

Solution 69

```
auto function(char &parameter_1, char parameter_2) {
  parameter_1 = 'w';
  char char_2{'e'};
  parameter_1 = 'b';
  auto &char_4 = parameter_1;
  parameter_2 = 'm';
  auto &char_6 = parameter_2;
  print("{}{}",
```

```cpp
                 char_6, char_2);
}
void run() {
  char char_1{'s'};
  auto &char_2 = char_1;
  auto char_3 = char_2;
  char char_4{'v'};
  char_2 = 'm';
  auto char_6 = char_4;
  char char_7{'r'};
  char_3 = 'g';
  char char_9{'o'};
  auto &char_10 = char_3;
  char_6 = 'f';
  char char_12{'c'};
  auto &char_13 = char_10;
  function(char_4, char_2);                    // me
  char char_14{'h'};
  print("{}{}{}{}",                            // mchr
        char_1, char_12, char_14, char_7);
}

// Answer: memchr
```

Solution 70

```cpp
auto function(char &parameter_1, char &parameter_2) {
  char char_1{'h'};
  auto char_2 = parameter_2;
  char char_3{'u'};
  auto &char_4 = char_1;
  char_1 = 'a';
  auto &char_6 = char_1;
  print("{}{}",
        char_1, char_2);
}
void run() {
  char char_1{'h'};
  auto char_2 = char_1;
  auto &char_3 = char_2;
  auto char_4 = char_1;
  char_3 = 'a';
  char char_6{'s'};
```

```cpp
  print("{}",                                    // s
        char_6);
  char_4 = 'y';
  char char_8{'s'};
  auto char_9 = char_8;
  char_3 = 'e';
  auto &char_11 = char_9;
  print("{}{}{}",                                // yse
        char_4, char_8, char_2);
  char_9 = 'r';
  char char_13{'.'};
  auto char_14 = char_3;
  char char_15{'h'};
  print("{}{}{}{}",                              // rr.h
        char_9, char_11, char_13, char_15);
  function(char_1, char_6);                      // as
  print("{}",                                    // h
        char_1);
}

// Answer: syserr.hash
```

Solution 71

```cpp
auto function(char &parameter_1, char parameter_2) {
  print("{}",
        parameter_1);
  parameter_2 = 'o';
  print("{}",
        parameter_2);
  parameter_2 = 'k';
  char char_3{'l'};
  auto char_4 = parameter_1;
  print("{}",
        char_4);
}
void run() {
  char char_1{'o'};
  auto char_2 = char_1;
  char char_3{'f'};
  auto &char_4 = char_3;
  char_2 = 'n';
  char char_6{'c'};
```

```
    char_4 = 'p';
    char char_8{'o'};
    auto char_9 = char_3;
    char char_10{'u'};
    function(char_3, char_10);                      // p
                                                    // o
                                                    // p

    char char_11{'y'};
    auto &char_12 = char_4;
    char_4 = 't';
    auto &char_14 = char_6;
    char_9 = 'a';
    auto char_16 = char_10;
    print("{}{}{}{}{}",                             // count
          char_14, char_8, char_10, char_2, char_12);
}


// Answer: popcount
```

Solution 72

```
auto function(char &parameter_1, char &parameter_2) {
  parameter_1 = 'Q';
  parameter_2 = 'g';
  char char_3{'o'};
  parameter_2 = 'V';
  char char_5{'V'};
  auto &char_6 = char_3;
  print("{}",
        parameter_2);
}
void run() {
  char char_1{'Q'};
  auto char_2 = char_1;
  auto &char_3 = char_2;
  char char_4{'V'};
  function(char_2, char_4);                         // V
  char char_5{'V'};
  char_3 = 'P';
  char char_7{'O'};
  auto &char_8 = char_4;
  char_4 = 'M';
  print("{}{}{}",                                   // PMO
```

```cpp
        char_3, char_8, char_7);
  char char_10{'s'};
  char_10 = 'f';
  auto char_12 = char_8;
  auto &char_13 = char_3;
  char_12 = '2';
  auto char_15 = char_12;
  char_13 = 'M';
  auto &char_17 = char_2;
  print("{}{}{}{}",                                    // VQ2M
        char_5, char_1, char_12, char_2);
}
```

```cpp
// Answer: VPMOVQ2M
```

Solution 73

```cpp
auto function(char &parameter_1, char parameter_2) {
  char char_1{'f'};
  auto &char_2 = char_1;
  char char_3{'m'};
  parameter_1 = 't';
  auto &char_5 = char_2;
  char_5 = 's';
  print("{}{}{}",
        char_1, parameter_1, char_3);
}
void run() {
  char char_1{'k'};
  char_1 = 'o';
  char char_3{'m'};
  char_1 = 't';
  auto char_5 = char_1;
  char char_6{'s'};
  auto &char_7 = char_5;
  auto char_8 = char_7;
  char_1 = '.';
  auto char_10 = char_1;
  auto &char_11 = char_7;
  char_10 = 't';
  function(char_11, char_6);                           // stm
  auto char_13 = char_1;
  char char_14{'p'};
```

```cpp
  auto &char_15 = char_11;
  char char_16{'t'};
  print("{}{}{}{}{}{}",                                  // t.stmt
        char_16, char_13, char_6, char_11, char_3, char_5);
}
```

```
// Answer: stmt.stmt
```

Solution 74

```cpp
auto function(char &parameter_1, char parameter_2) {
  parameter_2 = 's';
  char char_2{'l'};
  auto char_3 = parameter_2;
  char char_4{'c'};
  auto &char_5 = char_4;
  char char_6{'a'};
  print("{}{}{}",
        char_6, char_3, parameter_2);
}
void run() {
  char char_1{'s'};
  char_1 = 'l';
  char char_3{'c'};
  char_3 = 'c';
  auto &char_5 = char_3;
  char char_6{'a'};
  print("{}{}",                                          // cl
        char_5, char_1);
  auto char_7 = char_1;
  auto &char_8 = char_1;
  char char_9{'.'};
  char_8 = 'b';
  char char_11{'t'};
  function(char_7, char_6);                              // ass
  auto &char_12 = char_7;
  char char_13{'m'};
  char_8 = 'f';
  char char_15{'i'};
  auto &char_16 = char_1;
  print("{}{}{}{}{}",                                    // .mfct
        char_9, char_13, char_16, char_3, char_11);
}
```

```
// Answer: class.mfct
```

Solution 75

```
auto function(char parameter_1, char &parameter_2) {
  print("{}",
        parameter_2);
  char char_1{'o'};
  char_1 = 'h';
  auto &char_3 = parameter_1;
  parameter_1 = 'e';
  char char_5{'p'};
  print("{}{}",
        char_5, char_3);
}
void run() {
  char char_1{'o'};
  auto char_2 = char_1;
  char char_3{'x'};
  char_3 = 'e';
  char char_5{'p'};
  auto &char_6 = char_3;
  char_1 = 'r';
  function(char_1, char_2);                          // o
                                                     // pe

  char char_8{'n'};
  char_6 = 'e';
  auto char_10 = char_1;
  char char_11{'a'};
  char_3 = 'f';
  char char_13{'x'};
  char_1 = 't';
  char char_15{'h'};
  auto char_16 = char_10;
  auto &char_17 = char_6;
  auto char_18 = char_1;
  print("{}{}{}{}{}",                                // rator
        char_10, char_11, char_1, char_2, char_16);
}
```

```
// Answer: operator
```

Solution 76

```cpp
auto function(char parameter_1, char &parameter_2) {
  parameter_2 = 'i';
  parameter_1 = 'j';
  char char_3{'s'};
  print("{}",
        parameter_2);
  parameter_1 = 'd';
  char char_5{'x'};
  print("{}{}",
        char_3, char_5);
}
void run() {
  char char_1{'i'};
  auto char_2 = char_1;
  function(char_1, char_2);                        // i
                                                   // sx

  auto &char_3 = char_1;
  char char_4{'d'};
  char_2 = 'x';
  char char_6{'t'};
  auto char_7 = char_2;
  char char_8{'g'};
  auto &char_9 = char_3;
  char_7 = 'i';
  auto &char_11 = char_8;
  char_9 = 'q';
  auto &char_13 = char_6;
  auto char_14 = char_1;
  char_3 = 'i';
  char char_16{'e'};
  auto &char_17 = char_4;
  print("{}{}{}{}{}",                              // digit
        char_4, char_3, char_8, char_7, char_13);
}

// Answer: isxdigit
```

Solution 77

```cpp
auto function(char &parameter_1, char &parameter_2) {
  parameter_2 = 't';
  parameter_2 = 'f';
  char char_3{'s'};
  parameter_2 = 'a';
  char char_5{'y'};
  char_3 = 'x';
  print("{}",
        parameter_1);
}
void run() {
  char char_1{'b'};
  char_1 = 'c';
  auto &char_3 = char_1;
  char char_4{'a'};
  char_1 = 'd';
  function(char_1, char_3);                      // a
  auto &char_6 = char_1;
  auto char_7 = char_6;
  char char_8{'2'};
  auto &char_9 = char_7;
  char char_10{'n'};
  auto &char_11 = char_10;
  auto char_12 = char_10;
  char_3 = 'f';
  char char_14{'t'};
  auto char_15 = char_12;
  auto &char_16 = char_12;
  print("{}{}{}{}{}",                            // tan2f
        char_14, char_4, char_16, char_8, char_1);
}

// Answer: atan2f
```

Solution 78

```cpp
auto function(char &parameter_1, char parameter_2) {
  char char_1{'a'};
  char char_2{'f'};
  auto char_3 = parameter_2;
  char char_4{'p'};
  auto &char_5 = char_4;
  char_3 = 'o';
  print("{}{}{}",
        char_4, char_1, parameter_2);
}
void run() {
  char char_1{'a'};
  auto &char_2 = char_1;
  char_1 = 'd';
  auto char_4 = char_1;
  char_2 = 'n';
  char char_6{'o'};
  auto char_7 = char_1;
  char_1 = 'r';
  auto char_9 = char_4;
  auto &char_10 = char_2;
  char_4 = 't';
  function(char_9, char_2);                        // par
  char char_12{'i'};
  auto &char_13 = char_1;
  char char_14{'i'};
  auto &char_15 = char_12;
  char_14 = 'b';
  auto char_17 = char_9;
  char char_18{'t'};
  print("{}{}{}{}{}{}",                            // tition
        char_18, char_15, char_4, char_12, char_6, char_7);
}

// Answer: partition
```

Solution 79

```cpp
auto function(char &parameter_1, char &parameter_2) {
  char char_1{'r'};
  char_1 = 'r';
  auto &char_3 = parameter_2;
  parameter_1 = 'e';
  auto char_5 = parameter_2;
  char_3 = '.';
  print("{}{}{}",
        char_3, char_1, parameter_1);
}
void run() {
  char char_1{'r'};
  auto &char_2 = char_1;
  char char_3{'e'};
  print("{}{}",                                        // re
        char_2, char_3);
  auto &char_4 = char_2;
  auto char_5 = char_2;
  char_1 = '.';
  auto &char_7 = char_5;
  function(char_5, char_4);                            // .re
  auto char_8 = char_7;
  auto &char_9 = char_8;
  auto char_10 = char_9;
  auto &char_11 = char_9;
  char_4 = 'r';
  char char_13{'t'};
  auto &char_14 = char_10;
  char_14 = 'i';
  auto &char_16 = char_11;
  char char_17{'g'};
  print("{}{}{}{}{}",                                  // giter
        char_17, char_10, char_13, char_11, char_1);
}

// Answer: re.regiter
```

Solution 80

```cpp
auto function(char parameter_1, char &parameter_2) {
  parameter_1 = 'a';
  parameter_1 = 's';
  char char_3{'c'};
  auto char_4 = parameter_2;
  print("{}",
        parameter_1);
  auto &char_5 = char_3;
  print("{}",
        char_5);
}
void run() {
  char char_1{'a'};
  print("{}",                                // a
        char_1);
  char char_2{'s'};
  function(char_2, char_1);                  // s
                                             // c

  char_2 = 'c';
  auto char_4 = char_1;
  char_1 = 'v';
  auto &char_6 = char_4;
  char char_7{'t'};
  char_4 = 'i';
  char char_9{'e'};
  auto char_10 = char_4;
  auto &char_11 = char_6;
  char char_12{'y'};
  auto &char_13 = char_10;
  char char_14{'t'};
  char_2 = 'v';
  char char_16{'k'};
  char_2 = 'm';
  auto &char_18 = char_10;
  auto char_19 = char_11;
  print("{}{}{}{}",                          // time
        char_14, char_6, char_2, char_9);
}

// Answer: asctime
```

Solution 81

```
auto function(char &parameter_1, char parameter_2) {
  parameter_1 = 'e';
  print("{}",
        parameter_2);
  char char_2{'e'};
  auto &char_3 = char_2;
  char char_4{'y'};
  auto char_5 = char_4;
  print("{}",
        char_3);
}
void run() {
  char char_1{'u'};
  auto &char_2 = char_1;
  char_1 = 'g';
  char char_4{'g'};
  auto char_5 = char_1;
  char_4 = 'n';
  function(char_5, char_2);                              // g
                                                         // e

  char char_7{'a'};
  char_1 = 'h';
  auto char_9 = char_7;
  char char_10{'e'};
  char_9 = 'a';
  char char_12{'c'};
  char_10 = 'o';
  auto char_14 = char_10;
  char_2 = 'r';
  auto char_16 = char_1;
  auto &char_17 = char_9;
  char_5 = 'e';
  auto &char_19 = char_7;
  function(char_14, char_4);                             // n
                                                         // e

  auto &char_20 = char_14;
  char_4 = 't';
  auto char_22 = char_10;
  print("{}{}{}{}{}",                                    // rator
        char_1, char_7, char_4, char_22, char_16);
}
```

Solution 82

```
auto function(char &parameter_1, char parameter_2) {
  parameter_1 = 'l';
  print("{}",
        parameter_1);
  parameter_2 = 'u';
  char char_3{'g'};
  auto &char_4 = parameter_1;
  char char_5{'e'};
  print("{}{}",
        char_5, char_3);
}
void run() {
  char char_1{'l'};
  char_1 = 'k';
  char char_3{'g'};
  char_1 = 'l';
  function(char_1, char_3);                     // l
                                                // eg

  char char_5{'e'};
  auto char_6 = char_1;
  char char_7{'l'};
  char_6 = 'm';
  char char_9{'d'};
  auto char_10 = char_3;
  char char_11{'n'};
  auto char_12 = char_1;
  auto &char_13 = char_11;
  char_6 = 'r';
  char char_15{'q'};
  auto &char_16 = char_3;
  auto char_17 = char_5;
  char char_18{'k'};
  print("{}{}{}{}{}",                           // endre
        char_5, char_11, char_9, char_6, char_17);
}
```

Solution 83

```cpp
auto function(char &parameter_1, char &parameter_2) {
  parameter_1 = 'c';
  parameter_1 = '.';
  char char_3{'p'};
  auto &char_4 = char_3;
  print("{}",
        char_3);
  char char_5{'x'};
  print("{}{}",
        char_4, parameter_1);
}
void run() {
  char char_1{'c'};
  print("{}",                                  // c
        char_1);
  char_1 = '.';
  auto char_3 = char_1;
  char_3 = 'b';
  function(char_1, char_3);                     // p
                                                // p.

  auto &char_5 = char_3;
  char char_6{'k'};
  char_1 = 'r';
  auto char_8 = char_5;
  char char_9{'b'};
  auto char_10 = char_8;
  char_8 = 'e';
  char char_12{'r'};
  char_9 = 'o';
  auto char_14 = char_9;
  char char_15{'i'};
  char_15 = 'n';
  auto char_17 = char_1;
  auto &char_18 = char_8;
  auto char_19 = char_17;
  char char_20{'q'};
  auto &char_21 = char_12;
  print("{}{}{}{}{}",                           // error
        char_18, char_21, char_12, char_9, char_17);
}
```

```cpp
// Answer: cpp.error
```

Solution 84

```cpp
auto function(char parameter_1, char &parameter_2) {
  parameter_2 = 's';
  print("{}",
        parameter_2);
  char char_2{'t'};
  auto &char_3 = char_2;
  char char_4{'a'};
  parameter_2 = 'n';
  print("{}",
        char_3);
}
void run() {
  char char_1{'s'};
  print("{}",                               // s
        char_1);
  char char_2{'t'};
  auto &char_3 = char_2;
  char_2 = 'a';
  auto char_5 = char_3;
  auto &char_6 = char_5;
  char_6 = 'e';
  char char_8{'m'};
  auto char_9 = char_1;
  char char_10{'r'};
  char_5 = 's';
  auto char_12 = char_6;
  char char_13{'y'};
  auto &char_14 = char_12;
  auto char_15 = char_12;
  char char_16{'e'};
  char_6 = '.';
  auto char_18 = char_5;
  function(char_9, char_15);                // s
                                            // t

  char_18 = 'u';
  auto char_20 = char_13;
  print("{}{}{}{}{}{}{}{}",                 // ream.syn
        char_10, char_16, char_3, char_8, char_5, char_9,
        char_20, char_15);
```

```
}

// Answer: sstream.syn
```

Solution 85

```
auto function(char &parameter_1, char parameter_2) {
  parameter_1 = 'j';
  parameter_1 = 'b';
  char char_3{'f'};
  auto &char_4 = parameter_2;
  parameter_1 = 'p';
  auto char_6 = char_4;
  print("{}",
        char_6);
}
void run() {
  char char_1{'w'};
  auto &char_2 = char_1;
  char_1 = 'f';
  function(char_2, char_1);                      // f
  char_1 = 'e';
  auto char_5 = char_1;
  char char_6{'c'};
  print("{}",                                    // e
        char_1);
  auto &char_7 = char_6;
  char_5 = 'u';
  auto &char_9 = char_1;
  function(char_2, char_5);                      // u
  char_7 = 'e';
  char char_11{'f'};
  function(char_11, char_2);                     // p
  char_2 = 'd';
  function(char_11, char_1);                     // d
  auto char_13 = char_7;
  char char_14{'n'};
  char_5 = 'a';
  auto char_16 = char_1;
  function(char_16, char_5);                     // a
  auto &char_17 = char_1;
  char char_18{'t'};
  auto &char_19 = char_2;
```

```cpp
  auto char_20 = char_9;
  char_9 = 'v';
  char char_22{'i'};
  print("{}{}{}{}{}",                                    // teenv
        char_18, char_6, char_7, char_14, char_9);
}
```

```cpp
// Answer: feupdateenv
```

Solution 86

```cpp
auto function(char parameter_1, char &parameter_2) {
  char char_1{'o'};
  auto char_2 = parameter_1;
  auto &char_3 = parameter_1;
  auto char_4 = char_1;
  char char_5{'u'};
  auto char_6 = char_2;
  print("{}{}{}",
        char_3, char_4, char_6);
}
void run() {
  char char_1{'o'};
  char char_2{'.'};
  char_1 = 'w';
  auto &char_4 = char_2;
  auto char_5 = char_2;
  auto &char_6 = char_2;
  char char_7{'p'};
  auto &char_8 = char_6;
  function(char_7, char_2);                              // pop
  char_5 = 'e';
  auto &char_10 = char_1;
  char_1 = 'b';
  auto char_12 = char_6;
  char_1 = 'h';
  auto &char_14 = char_2;
  auto char_15 = char_10;
  char char_16{'w'};
  auto char_17 = char_8;
  char char_18{'a'};
  char_16 = 'b';
  auto char_20 = char_4;
```

```
  print("{}{}{}{}{}",                                    // .heap
        char_12, char_1, char_5, char_18, char_7);
}


// Answer: pop.heap
```

Solution 87

```
auto function(char &parameter_1, char parameter_2) {
  parameter_1 = 'j';
  char char_2{'x'};
  parameter_1 = 'f';
  auto char_4 = char_2;
  parameter_1 = 'm';
  char char_6{'c'};
  print("{}{}",
        char_6, parameter_2);
}
void run() {
  char char_1{'b'};
  auto char_2 = char_1;
  char char_3{'t'};
  char_2 = 'e';
  auto char_5 = char_2;
  char_3 = 'c';
  auto char_7 = char_5;
  char_5 = 'o';
  char char_9{'y'};
  auto &char_10 = char_7;
  char_3 = 'r';
  auto char_12 = char_3;
  char_3 = 'n';
  char char_14{'t'};
  auto &char_15 = char_12;
  char char_16{'i'};
  function(char_1, char_5);                              // co
  auto char_17 = char_12;
  auto &char_18 = char_14;
  char char_19{'i'};
  auto &char_20 = char_2;
  char char_21{'u'};
  print("{}{}{}{}{}{}{}",                                // routine
        char_15, char_5, char_21, char_14, char_16, char_3,
```

```
      char_2);
}


// Answer: coroutine
```

Solution 88

```
auto function(char &parameter_1, char parameter_2) {
  parameter_1 = 'e';
  char char_2{'e'};
  auto &char_3 = char_2;
  auto char_4 = char_2;
  char char_5{'u'};
  auto char_6 = char_5;
  print("{}{}{}",
        parameter_2, parameter_1, char_2);
}
void run() {
  char char_1{'e'};
  auto &char_2 = char_1;
  auto char_3 = char_1;
  char_1 = 's';
  auto char_5 = char_3;
  auto &char_6 = char_5;
  char_6 = 'y';
  auto char_8 = char_2;
  auto &char_9 = char_1;
  auto char_10 = char_2;
  char char_11{'f'};
  function(char_1, char_8);                      // see
  auto char_12 = char_1;
  char_5 = 'u';
  auto char_14 = char_2;
  char char_15{'_'};
  auto &char_16 = char_11;
  char_1 = 'q';
  char char_18{'v'};
  char_5 = 'd';
  auto &char_20 = char_16;
  char_18 = 's';
  char char_22{'i'};
  print("{}{}{}{}{}",                            // d_seq
        char_6, char_15, char_18, char_12, char_2);
```

```
}

// Answer: seed_seq
```

Solution 89

```
auto function(char &parameter_1, char parameter_2) {
  parameter_1 = 's';
  parameter_2 = 'c';
  print("{}",
        parameter_2);
  char char_3{'l'};
  auto &char_4 = parameter_2;
  char_4 = 'l';
  print("{}",
        char_3);
}
void run() {
  char char_1{'s'};
  auto char_2 = char_1;
  char_1 = 'l';
  auto char_4 = char_1;
  char_4 = 'y';
  auto &char_6 = char_4;
  char char_7{'a'};
  auto char_8 = char_7;
  char char_9{'x'};
  char_6 = 'f';
  auto &char_11 = char_6;
  function(char_4, char_9);                          // c
                                                     // l

  char char_12{'l'};
  auto char_13 = char_6;
  char_12 = 'e';
  auto char_15 = char_6;
  char char_16{'q'};
  auto char_17 = char_16;
  auto &char_18 = char_17;
  char_17 = '.';
  auto char_20 = char_16;
  char char_21{'s'};
  print("{}{}{}{}{}{}",                              // ass.eq
        char_8, char_2, char_6, char_18, char_12, char_20);
```

```
}

// Answer: class.eq
```

Solution 90

```
auto function(char &parameter_1, char parameter_2) {
  char char_1{'f'};
  char_1 = 'e';
  print("{}",
        parameter_2);
  parameter_1 = 'd';
  auto char_4 = parameter_1;
  char char_5{'u'};
  print("{}",
        char_4);
}
void run() {
  char char_1{'y'};
  char_1 = 'e';
  auto &char_3 = char_1;
  auto char_4 = char_1;
  char_1 = 'u';
  char char_6{'q'};
  auto char_7 = char_4;
  print("{}",                                   // q
        char_6);
  auto &char_8 = char_4;
  print("{}{}",                                 // ue
        char_1, char_4);
  auto char_9 = char_8;
  print("{}{}",                                 // ue
        char_3, char_7);
  auto &char_10 = char_4;
  auto char_11 = char_9;
  char_6 = '.';
  auto char_13 = char_9;
  char_10 = 'n';
  auto &char_15 = char_9;
  function(char_1, char_6);                     // .
                                                // d

  char char_16{'o'};
  char_6 = 's';
```

```
    auto &char_18 = char_4;
    char char_19{'k'};
    auto char_20 = char_19;
    char char_21{'f'};
    print("{}{}{}",                                        // efn
          char_11, char_21, char_18);
}

// Answer: queue.defn
```

Solution 91

```
auto function(char &parameter_1, char &parameter_2) {
  char char_1{'m'};
  auto char_2 = parameter_1;
  parameter_1 = 'n';
  char char_4{'i'};
  print("{}",
        char_1);
  char char_5{'e'};
  print("{}",
        char_5);
}
void run() {
  char char_1{'m'};
  auto &char_2 = char_1;
  char_1 = 'n';
  auto char_4 = char_2;
  char_1 = 'e';
  char char_6{'r'};
  auto &char_7 = char_4;
  auto char_8 = char_6;
  auto &char_9 = char_6;
  char char_10{'r'};
  auto &char_11 = char_7;
  char char_12{'s'};
  function(char_6, char_9);                               // m
                                                          // e

  char char_13{'v'};
  auto &char_14 = char_8;
  auto char_15 = char_7;
  auto &char_16 = char_6;
  char_15 = 'i';
```

```cpp
  auto char_18 = char_2;
  char char_19{'g'};
  auto char_20 = char_1;
  print("{}{}{}{}{}{}",                              // rsenne
        char_8, char_12, char_2, char_16, char_6, char_20);
}

// Answer: mersenne
```

Solution 92

```cpp
auto function(char parameter_1, char &parameter_2) {
  char char_1{'q'};
  auto char_2 = parameter_1;
  parameter_2 = 'q';
  auto char_4 = char_2;
  char char_5{'t'};
  auto char_6 = char_1;
  print("{}{}",
        char_4, char_5);
}
void run() {
  char char_1{'o'};
  char_1 = 't';
  auto &char_3 = char_1;
  char_1 = 's';
  auto char_5 = char_3;
  function(char_3, char_1);                          // st
  char char_6{'m'};
  auto &char_7 = char_5;
  function(char_6, char_3);                          // mt
  auto &char_8 = char_3;
  char_3 = '.';
  auto char_10 = char_6;
  auto &char_11 = char_8;
  char char_12{'k'};
  char_7 = 'u';
  auto &char_14 = char_6;
  char char_15{'p'};
  auto char_16 = char_7;
  char char_17{'o'};
  char_17 = 'i';
  auto char_19 = char_16;
```

```
  char char_20{'n'};
  char_16 = 'j';
  auto char_22 = char_15;
  auto &char_23 = char_1;
  print("{}{}{}{}{}",                                      // .jump
        char_11, char_16, char_5, char_10, char_22);
}


// Answer: stmt.jump
```

Solution 93

```
auto function(char parameter_1, char &parameter_2) {
  char char_1{'c'};
  parameter_2 = 'l';
  auto char_3 = parameter_1;
  print("{}{}",
        char_1, parameter_2);
  char_1 = 'e';
  char char_5{'b'};
  print("{}",
        parameter_1);
}
void run() {
  char char_1{'c'};
  char_1 = 'l';
  char char_3{'e'};
  char_1 = 'h';
  function(char_3, char_1);                          // cl
                                                     // e

  char char_5{'k'};
  auto &char_6 = char_5;
  char_5 = 'x';
  char char_8{'f'};
  char_6 = 'k';
  char char_10{'c'};
  auto &char_11 = char_5;
  char_5 = 't';
  auto char_13 = char_8;
  char_10 = 'r';
  char char_15{'v'};
  char_5 = 'r';
  char char_17{'y'};
```

```
    auto char_18 = char_3;
    char char_19{'a'};
    auto char_20 = char_5;
    char char_21{'j'};
    auto &char_22 = char_15;
    auto char_23 = char_11;
    char_17 = 'r';
    auto &char_25 = char_19;
    print("{}{}{}{}{}",                          // arerr
          char_19, char_10, char_18, char_17, char_5);
}

// Answer: clearerr
```

Solution 94

```
auto function(char parameter_1, char &parameter_2) {
  parameter_2 = 'q';
  parameter_2 = 'u';
  print("{}",
        parameter_2);
  char char_3{'v'};
  auto &char_4 = parameter_2;
  char char_5{'e'};
  print("{}",
        char_5);
}
void run() {
  char char_1{'q'};
  char char_2{'u'};
  print("{}",                                   // q
        char_1);
  auto &char_3 = char_2;
  char char_4{'o'};
  auto &char_5 = char_1;
  auto char_6 = char_4;
  char char_7{'i'};
  auto &char_8 = char_6;
  function(char_2, char_4);                      // u
                                                 // e
  char_4 = 'o';
  auto char_10 = char_6;
  char char_11{'s'};
```

```cpp
  auto char_12 = char_11;
  char char_13{'.'};
  char_3 = 'o';
  auto char_15 = char_11;
  function(char_3, char_7);                              // u
                                                         // e

  char_7 = 'c';
  char char_17{'c'};
  auto &char_18 = char_2;
  char char_19{'n'};
  char_5 = 'x';
  auto char_21 = char_15;
  print("{}{}{}{}{}",                                    // .cons
        char_13, char_17, char_2, char_19, char_11);
}

// Answer: queue.cons
```

Solution 95

```cpp
auto function(char &parameter_1, char parameter_2) {
  parameter_1 = 'h';
  char char_2{'r'};
  parameter_2 = 'e';
  auto char_4 = parameter_2;
  char char_5{'a'};
  parameter_1 = 'g';
  print("{}{}",
        char_2, parameter_2);
}
void run() {
  char char_1{'a'};
  char_1 = 'r';
  auto char_3 = char_1;
  char char_4{'y'};
  char_1 = 'a';
  auto &char_6 = char_4;
  auto char_7 = char_3;
  char char_8{'m'};
  auto char_9 = char_4;
  char_9 = 'e';
  auto char_11 = char_8;
  char char_12{'.'};
```

```cpp
  auto &char_13 = char_11;
  auto char_14 = char_11;
  function(char_3, char_14);                          // re
  char char_15{'l'};
  char_9 = 'a';
  auto char_17 = char_4;
  char_14 = 'r';
  auto char_19 = char_4;
  char_6 = 's';
  char char_21{'r'};
  auto &char_22 = char_3;
  char char_23{'n'};
  auto char_24 = char_22;
  print("{}{}{}{}{}{}{}{}",                            // .grammar
        char_12, char_22, char_21, char_9, char_13, char_8,
        char_1, char_7);
}

// Answer: re.grammar
```

Solution 96

```cpp
auto function(char &parameter_1, char parameter_2) {
  parameter_1 = 'k';
  parameter_2 = 't';
  print("{}",
        parameter_2);
  char char_3{'i'};
  auto char_4 = char_3;
  print("{}",
        char_4);
}
void run() {
  char char_1{'t'};
  char_1 = 't';
  auto char_3 = char_1;
  char char_4{'d'};
  auto char_5 = char_1;
  function(char_1, char_3);                            // t
                                                       // i

  char char_6{'a'};
  auto &char_7 = char_3;
  char char_8{'b'};
```

```
  char_5 = 'v';
  auto &char_10 = char_4;
  auto char_11 = char_10;
  char_11 = 'e';
  auto &char_13 = char_11;
  char char_14{'s'};
  auto &char_15 = char_13;
  char char_16{'d'};
  auto &char_17 = char_1;
  auto char_18 = char_14;
  char_3 = 'm';
  auto char_20 = char_6;
  char char_21{'_'};
  auto &char_22 = char_7;
  print("{}{}{}{}{}{}{}",                              // me_base
        char_22, char_11, char_21, char_8, char_20, char_18,
        char_13);
}


// Answer: time_base
```

Solution 97

```
void run() {
  char char_1{'n'};
  auto char_2 = char_1;
  char_2 = 'P';
  char char_4{'A'};
  auto char_5 = char_2;
  print("{}",                                          // P
        char_5);
  auto &char_6 = char_5;
  char_5 = 'D';
  auto char_8 = char_5;
  print("{}{}",                                        // AD
        char_4, char_6);
  auto char_9 = char_6;
  char_8 = 'Q';
  auto &char_11 = char_1;
  char_6 = 'y';
  auto char_13 = char_11;
  auto &char_14 = char_4;
  print("{}{}",                                        // DQ
```

```
        char_9, char_8);
}
```


Solution 98

```cpp
void run() {
  char char_1{'u'};
  char_1 = 'a';
  auto &char_3 = char_1;
  auto char_4 = char_1;
  auto &char_5 = char_3;
  auto char_6 = char_1;
  char_5 = 'l';
  char char_8{'a'};
  auto &char_9 = char_6;
  auto char_10 = char_1;
  char_10 = 'C';
  auto char_12 = char_3;
  char_9 = 'e';
  print("{}{}{}{}",                         // Call
        char_10, char_8, char_1, char_5);
  char char_14{'b'};
  auto char_15 = char_14;
  print("{}{}{}{}",                         // able
        char_4, char_15, char_3, char_6);
}
```


Solution 99

```cpp
void run() {
  char char_1{'j'};
  auto &char_2 = char_1;
  char_1 = 'i';
  std::swap(char_2, char_1);
  auto char_4 = char_2;
  char_1 = 'f';
  auto char_6 = char_4;
  char char_7{'d'};
  std::swap(char_7, char_6);
```

```cpp
    char char_8{'g'};
    std::swap(char_8, char_6);
    print("{}{}",                                    // di
        char_8, char_7);
    char_7 = 'j';
    char char_10{'p'};
    print("{}",                                      // f
        char_2);
    char_6 = 'e';
    std::swap(char_8, char_6);
    print("{}",                                      // f
        char_1);
    auto char_12 = char_7;
    char char_13{'e'};
    std::swap(char_7, char_2);
    char_12 = 'm';
    auto char_15 = char_7;
    char char_16{'p'};
    auto &char_17 = char_13;
    char char_18{'t'};
    print("{}{}{}{}",                                // time
        char_18, char_4, char_12, char_17);
}

// Answer: difftime
```

Solution 100

```cpp
void run() {
  char char_1{'e'};
  char char_2{'i'};
  auto char_3 = char_2;
  print("{}",                                        // i
      char_3);
  char char_4{'e'};
  auto char_5 = char_4;
  char char_6{'s'};
  auto char_7 = char_5;
  std::swap(char_2, char_3);
  char char_8{'l'};
  char_2 = 's';
  auto char_10 = char_7;
  auto &char_11 = char_6;
```

```cpp
  char_2 = 'e';
  std::swap(char_8, char_3);
  char_5 = 'l';
  auto char_14 = char_6;
  std::swap(char_14, char_10);
  auto char_15 = char_11;
  char char_16{'l'};
  auto &char_17 = char_10;
  print("{}{}{}{}{}",                        // sless
        char_10, char_16, char_4, char_17, char_15);
}

// Answer: isless
```

Solution 101

```cpp
void run() {
  char char_1{'e'};
  auto char_2 = char_1;
  auto &char_3 = char_2;
  char char_4{'c'};
  char_2 = 'w';
  char char_6{'c'};
  char_1 = 't';
  auto &char_8 = char_6;
  char char_9{'w'};
  print("{}{}",                              // wc
        char_9, char_6);
  char_4 = 'f';
  char char_11{'x'};
  auto &char_12 = char_1;
  char_3 = 'y';
  char char_14{'p'};
  auto char_15 = char_9;
  std::swap(char_11, char_9);
  auto &char_16 = char_14;
  char char_17{'e'};
  auto char_18 = char_9;
  auto &char_19 = char_14;
  auto char_20 = char_14;
  print("{}{}{}{}",                          // type
        char_12, char_3, char_14, char_17);
}
```

```
// Answer: wctype
```

Solution 102

```cpp
void run() {
  char char_1{'s'};
  char_1 = 'x';
  char char_3{'n'};
  auto &char_4 = char_3;
  char char_5{'j'};
  auto char_6 = char_5;
  char_4 = 'e';
  auto char_8 = char_4;
  char char_9{'w'};
  char_8 = 'j';
  auto &char_11 = char_9;
  char char_12{'O'};
  char_5 = '2';
  auto &char_14 = char_6;
  char_8 = 'M';
  auto char_16 = char_8;
  char char_17{'w'};
  auto &char_18 = char_14;
  char_6 = 'V';
  auto char_20 = char_18;
  std::swap(char_1, char_5);
  char_8 = 'M';
  auto &char_22 = char_12;
  char char_23{'P'};
  char_11 = 'B';
  std::swap(char_9, char_4);
  auto char_25 = char_8;
  print("{}{}{}{}{}{}{}{}",                       // VPMOVB2M
        char_14, char_23, char_8, char_22, char_20, char_4,
        char_1, char_16);
}
```

```
// Answer: VPMOVB2M
```

Solution 103

```cpp
void run() {
  char char_1{'D'};
  auto char_2 = char_1;
  char char_3{'d'};
  auto char_4 = char_3;
  auto &char_5 = char_3;
  char char_6{'A'};
  char_4 = 'w';
  auto &char_8 = char_1;
  char_2 = 'a';
  char char_10{'-'};
  auto &char_11 = char_2;
  auto char_12 = char_6;
  std::swap(char_1, char_8);
  auto &char_13 = char_11;
  auto char_14 = char_5;
  auto &char_15 = char_4;
  char char_16{'x'};
  char_15 = 'c';
  std::swap(char_13, char_4);
  auto &char_18 = char_15;
  auto char_19 = char_3;
  std::swap(char_1, char_18);
  char char_20{'A'};
  char_6 = 'i';
  auto char_22 = char_5;
  char char_23{'D'};
  print("{}{}{}{}{}{}{}",                       // ADD-Add
        char_20, char_23, char_15, char_10, char_12, char_3,
        char_14);
}

// Answer: ADD-Add
```

Solution 104

```cpp
void run() {
  char char_1{'p'};
  auto char_2 = char_1;
  auto &char_3 = char_1;
  char_2 = 'l';
  char char_5{'c'};
  char_1 = 'o';
  auto char_7 = char_3;
  char char_8{'p'};
  char_8 = 't';
  auto &char_10 = char_2;
  char_7 = '_';
  char char_12{'m'};
  auto &char_13 = char_7;
  char char_14{'y'};
  char_2 = 'm';
  print("{}{}{}{}{}",                      // commo
        char_5, char_3, char_12, char_2, char_1);
  char char_16{'d'};
  char_16 = 'd';
  std::swap(char_13, char_7);
  char_1 = 'p';
  auto char_19 = char_8;
  char char_20{'n'};
  auto char_21 = char_13;
  auto &char_22 = char_1;
  char char_23{'t'};
  print("{}{}{}{}",                        // n_ty
        char_20, char_13, char_19, char_14);
  std::swap(char_10, char_3);
  char char_24{'y'};
  auto &char_25 = char_7;
  char char_26{'e'};
  char_1 = 'c';
  auto char_28 = char_10;
  print("{}{}{}{}",                        // pe_t
        char_28, char_26, char_7, char_23);
}


// Answer: common_type_t
```

Solution 105

```cpp
auto function(char &parameter_1, char parameter_2) {
  parameter_1 = 'f';
  parameter_2 = 'a';
  char char_3{'s'};
  print("{}",
        char_3);
  auto &char_4 = char_3;
  char char_5{'m'};
  print("{}",
        parameter_2);
}
void run() {
  char char_1{'o'};
  auto char_2 = char_1;
  char char_3{'s'};
  auto char_4 = char_1;
  char_4 = 'm';
  char char_6{'l'};
  auto &char_7 = char_1;
  char char_8{'j'};
  auto &char_9 = char_2;
  char_7 = 'p';
  function(char_3, char_8);                   // s
                                              // a
  char char_11{'e'};
  auto &char_12 = char_3;
  print("{}{}{}{}",                           // mple
        char_4, char_7, char_6, char_11);
}

// Answer: sample
```

Solution 106

```cpp
auto function(char &parameter_1, char parameter_2) {
  print("{}",
        parameter_1);
  parameter_2 = 'O';
  char char_2{'U'};
  auto &char_3 = char_2;
  parameter_1 = 'x';
  char char_5{'r'};
  print("{}",
        char_3);
}
void run() {
  char char_1{'O'};
  auto char_2 = char_1;
  char char_3{'W'};
  auto &char_4 = char_1;
  char_2 = 'y';
  std::swap(char_2, char_1);
  function(char_2, char_3);                      // O
                                                 // U

  auto &char_6 = char_4;
  char_4 = 'T';
  auto &char_8 = char_6;
  char char_9{'S'};
  auto char_10 = char_3;
  auto &char_11 = char_1;
  std::swap(char_9, char_8);
  auto &char_12 = char_9;
  print("{}{}{}",                                // TSW
        char_9, char_6, char_3);
}

// Answer: OUTSW
```

Solution 107

```cpp
auto function(char &parameter_1, char &parameter_2) {
  parameter_1 = 'l';
  parameter_2 = 'm';
  print("{}",
        parameter_2);
  parameter_1 = 'e';
  std::swap(parameter_2, parameter_1);
  char char_4{'a'};
  print("{}",
        char_4);
}
void run() {
  char char_1{'h'};
  auto &char_2 = char_1;
  auto char_3 = char_1;
  std::swap(char_1, char_3);
  char_1 = 'a';
  char char_5{'F'};
  auto &char_6 = char_2;
  char_1 = 'o';
  char char_8{'r'};
  auto &char_9 = char_6;
  print("{}{}{}",                          // For
        char_5, char_6, char_8);
  function(char_9, char_6);                // m
                                           // a
  auto char_10 = char_6;
  char char_11{'e'};
  auto &char_12 = char_11;
  std::swap(char_8, char_2);
  char_11 = 't';
  auto &char_14 = char_9;
  print("{}{}{}{}",                        // tter
        char_11, char_12, char_10, char_2);
}

// Answer: Formatter
```

Solution 108

```cpp
auto function(char parameter_1, char &parameter_2) {
  char char_1{'p'};
  parameter_2 = '.';
  char char_3{'t'};
  auto char_4 = parameter_1;
  char char_5{'e'};
  char_1 = 'p';
  print("{}{}",
        char_3, char_5);
}
void run() {
  char char_1{'q'};
  auto &char_2 = char_1;
  char_2 = 't';
  std::swap(char_1, char_2);
  char char_4{'m'};
  function(char_1, char_2);                     // te
  std::swap(char_4, char_2);
  auto char_5 = char_4;
  char char_6{'p'};
  auto &char_7 = char_1;
  auto char_8 = char_1;
  char_8 = 'r';
  char char_10{'p'};
  auto &char_11 = char_6;
  print("{}{}{}{}",                             // mp.p
        char_1, char_10, char_4, char_6);
  char_11 = 'w';
  auto &char_13 = char_6;
  char_13 = 'a';
  auto &char_15 = char_13;
  print("{}{}{}{}",                             // aram
        char_13, char_8, char_11, char_2);
}

// Answer: temp.param
```

Solution 109

```cpp
auto function(char parameter_1, char &parameter_2) {
  parameter_2 = 'P';
  parameter_2 = 'W';
  char char_3{'o'};
  char_3 = 'j';
  auto char_5 = char_3;
  std::swap(parameter_1, char_3);
  print("{}",
        char_3);
}
void run() {
  char char_1{'P'};
  auto &char_2 = char_1;
  auto char_3 = char_1;
  char char_4{'d'};
  char_4 = 'S';
  print("{}",                                // P
        char_3);
  char char_6{'o'};
  function(char_4, char_3);                   // S
  char char_7{'k'};
  char_1 = 'U';
  auto char_9 = char_1;
  function(char_2, char_6);                   // U
  char char_10{'B'};
  auto char_11 = char_10;
  char char_12{'g'};
  auto &char_13 = char_9;
  char char_14{'U'};
  print("{}{}{}{}",                           // BUSW
        char_10, char_14, char_4, char_6);
}

// Answer: PSUBUSW
```

Solution 110

```cpp
auto function(char parameter_1, char &parameter_2) {
  parameter_2 = 'l';
  std::swap(parameter_2, parameter_1);
  parameter_2 = 'f';
  char char_3{'r'};
  auto &char_4 = char_3;
  auto char_5 = parameter_2;
  print("{}",
        char_3);
}
void run() {
  char char_1{'t'};
  auto char_2 = char_1;
  char_2 = 'r';
  auto &char_4 = char_1;
  auto char_5 = char_4;
  function(char_1, char_2);                    // r
  auto &char_6 = char_5;
  char char_7{'x'};
  char_6 = 'e';
  auto char_9 = char_1;
  char_4 = 'e';
  auto &char_11 = char_6;
  print("{}{}{}",                              // efe
        char_6, char_2, char_1);
  function(char_7, char_6);                    // r
  auto char_12 = char_4;
  char_5 = 'c';
  char char_14{'n'};
  auto &char_15 = char_6;
  char_9 = 'k';
  char char_17{'e'};
  print("{}{}{}{}",                            // ence
        char_17, char_14, char_5, char_12);
}

// Answer: reference
```

Solution 111

```cpp
auto function(char &parameter_1, char parameter_2) {
  parameter_2 = 'c';
  char char_2{'u'};
  auto &char_3 = parameter_2;
  parameter_2 = '.';
  char char_5{'s'};
  auto char_6 = char_5;
  print("{}{}{}",
        char_5, char_6, parameter_2);
}
void run() {
  char char_1{'c'};
  char char_2{'q'};
  char_2 = 'a';
  print("{}",                                    // c
        char_1);
  std::swap(char_2, char_1);
  char char_4{'.'};
  char_2 = 's';
  auto &char_6 = char_1;
  char_2 = 'l';
  print("{}{}",                                  // la
        char_2, char_6);
  char char_8{'g'};
  auto char_9 = char_8;
  std::swap(char_2, char_1);
  char char_10{'h'};
  char_2 = 's';
  auto char_12 = char_1;
  char_10 = 'c';
  auto &char_14 = char_1;
  std::swap(char_10, char_9);
  char char_15{'e'};
  auto &char_16 = char_2;
  function(char_15, char_14);                    // ss.
  auto &char_17 = char_8;
  char char_18{'i'};
  print("{}{}{}{}{}{}",                          // gslice
        char_17, char_16, char_12, char_18, char_9, char_15);
}
```

```
// Answer: class.gslice
```

Solution 112

```
auto function(char &parameter_1, char &parameter_2) {
  char char_1{'c'};
  auto char_2 = char_1;
  auto &char_3 = char_2;
  char_3 = 'd';
  auto &char_5 = char_2;
  auto char_6 = char_5;
  print("{}{}",
        char_3, parameter_2);
}
void run() {
  char char_1{'c'};
  auto char_2 = char_1;
  auto &char_3 = char_1;
  function(char_3, char_2);                          // dc
  auto &char_4 = char_2;
  char char_5{'f'};
  auto char_6 = char_3;
  auto &char_7 = char_2;
  auto char_8 = char_6;
  char char_9{'v'};
  char_6 = 'd';
  auto &char_11 = char_7;
  char char_12{'c'};
  char_2 = 'l';
  auto &char_14 = char_3;
  char_5 = '.';
  char char_16{'q'};
  print("{}{}{}{}{}",                                // l.dcl
        char_7, char_5, char_6, char_3, char_4);
}

// Answer: dcl.dcl
```

Solution 113

```cpp
auto function(char parameter_1, char &parameter_2) {
  parameter_1 = 'd';
  parameter_2 = 'v';
  char char_3{'a'};
  parameter_1 = 'i';
  char char_5{'p'};
  print("{}{}",
        parameter_2, char_3);
}
void run() {
  char char_1{'d'};
  auto char_2 = char_1;
  char_2 = 'a';
  auto &char_4 = char_2;
  print("{}{}",                             // ad
        char_4, char_1);
  auto &char_5 = char_2;
  char char_6{'s'};
  auto &char_7 = char_5;
  char_5 = 'k';
  auto &char_9 = char_4;
  char_9 = 'c';
  char char_11{'y'};
  char_6 = 'e';
  function(char_5, char_4);                 // va
  char char_13{'a'};
  char_2 = 'c';
  auto char_15 = char_9;
  char char_16{'n'};
  auto char_17 = char_9;
  auto &char_18 = char_17;
  print("{}{}{}",                           // nce
        char_16, char_7, char_6);
}

// Answer: advance
```

Solution 114

```cpp
auto function(char &parameter_1, char &parameter_2) {
  char char_1{'g'};
  print("{}{}",
        parameter_2, char_1);
  auto char_2 = parameter_2;
  parameter_2 = 'j';
  char char_4{'u'};
  print("{}{}",
        char_4, parameter_1);
}
void run() {
  char char_1{'g'};
  char_1 = 'l';
  char char_3{'k'};
  print("{}",                                      // l
        char_1);
  auto &char_4 = char_3;
  char_3 = 'e';
  auto char_6 = char_4;
  char_1 = 'a';
  function(char_6, char_1);                         // ag
                                                    // ue

  char_6 = 'l';
  auto &char_9 = char_1;
  char_9 = 'r';
  auto char_11 = char_3;
  std::swap(char_4, char_1);
  auto char_12 = char_9;
  char_12 = 'e';
  auto char_14 = char_4;
  auto &char_15 = char_14;
  auto char_16 = char_11;
  char char_17{'x'};
  auto &char_18 = char_17;
  std::swap(char_17, char_4);
  auto &char_19 = char_12;
  auto char_20 = char_3;
  print("{}{}{}{}",                                 // rrel
        char_17, char_15, char_12, char_6);
}
```

```cpp
// Answer: laguerrel
```

Solution 115

```cpp
auto function(char &parameter_1, char parameter_2) {
  std::swap(parameter_1, parameter_2);
  parameter_1 = 'e';
  char char_2{'x'};
  auto char_3 = parameter_1;
  auto &char_4 = char_3;
  char_3 = 'p';
  print("{}{}",
        parameter_1, char_2);
}
void run() {
  char char_1{'e'};
  auto char_2 = char_1;
  auto &char_3 = char_1;
  auto char_4 = char_3;
  char char_5{'p'};
  char_1 = 'q';
  char char_7{'c'};
  char_3 = 'q';
  std::swap(char_5, char_1);
  auto char_9 = char_3;
  char_4 = '.';
  auto char_11 = char_4;
  char char_12{'r'};
  char_1 = 'd';
  function(char_1, char_7);                       // ex
  auto char_14 = char_12;
  char char_15{'j'};
  auto char_16 = char_4;
  auto &char_17 = char_9;
  char_16 = 'f';
  auto char_19 = char_14;
  print("{}{}{}{}{}{}",                           // pr.pre
        char_9, char_14, char_11, char_17, char_12, char_2);
}
```

```cpp
// Answer: expr.pre
```

Solution 116

```cpp
auto function(char parameter_1, char &parameter_2) {
  parameter_1 = 'e';
  print("{}",
        parameter_2);
  parameter_1 = 'l';
  print("{}",
        parameter_1);
  std::swap(parameter_2, parameter_1);
  parameter_2 = 'c';
}
void run() {
  char char_1{'e'};
  print("{}",                                     // e
        char_1);
  char_1 = 'l';
  auto char_3 = char_1;
  auto &char_4 = char_1;
  char_4 = 'r';
  char char_6{'g'};
  char_6 = 'v';
  auto &char_8 = char_4;
  char_8 = 'l';
  auto &char_10 = char_1;
  function(char_10, char_4);                       // l
                                                   // l
  auto char_11 = char_4;
  auto &char_12 = char_4;
  char char_13{'_'};
  auto &char_14 = char_8;
  char char_15{'2'};
  auto char_16 = char_6;
  char_12 = 't';
  char char_18{'n'};
  std::swap(char_12, char_15);
  auto char_19 = char_15;
  char char_20{'i'};
  print("{}{}{}{}{}{}",                            // int_2l
        char_20, char_18, char_15, char_13, char_4, char_3);
}

// Answer: ellint_2l
```

Solution 117

```cpp
auto function(char &parameter_1, char parameter_2) {
  parameter_2 = 's';
  print("{}",
        parameter_1);
  parameter_1 = 'u';
  char char_3{'x'};
  char_3 = 't';
  auto &char_5 = char_3;
  print("{}",
        char_3);
}
void run() {
  char char_1{'s'};
  auto char_2 = char_1;
  char char_3{'x'};
  function(char_1, char_2);                       // s
                                                  // t

  auto &char_4 = char_1;
  char_2 = 'r';
  function(char_2, char_4);                       // r
                                                  // t

  auto &char_6 = char_2;
  char char_7{'a'};
  std::swap(char_1, char_7);
  auto &char_8 = char_7;
  auto char_9 = char_3;
  char_7 = 'o';
  char char_11{'y'};
  auto char_12 = char_8;
  auto &char_13 = char_6;
  char char_14{'m'};
  char_11 = 'v';
  auto &char_16 = char_7;
  auto char_17 = char_12;
  char char_18{'k'};
  print("{}{}{}{}{}",                             // oumax
        char_12, char_6, char_14, char_4, char_9);
}

// Answer: strtoumax
```

Solution 118

```cpp
auto function(char &parameter_1, char parameter_2) {
  char char_1{'k'};
  parameter_2 = 'f';
  auto char_3 = parameter_1;
  std::swap(char_3, parameter_2);
  parameter_2 = 'n';
  char char_5{'l'};
  print("{}",
        char_5);
}
void run() {
  char char_1{'p'};
  auto &char_2 = char_1;
  char char_3{'s'};
  auto &char_4 = char_1;
  auto char_5 = char_4;
  auto &char_6 = char_3;
  char char_7{'o'};
  char_3 = 'd';
  function(char_5, char_4);                        // l
  char char_9{'u'};
  auto &char_10 = char_1;
  std::swap(char_1, char_5);
  char char_11{'t'};
  auto char_12 = char_6;
  char_4 = 'n';
  char char_14{'w'};
  function(char_7, char_1);                        // l
  auto char_15 = char_3;
  std::swap(char_4, char_3);
  char char_16{'r'};
  auto char_17 = char_16;
  auto &char_18 = char_3;
  print("{}{}{}{}{}",                              // round
        char_17, char_7, char_9, char_18, char_2);
}

// Answer: llround
```

Solution 119

```cpp
auto function(char &parameter_1, char &parameter_2) {
  print("{}",
        parameter_1);
  char char_1{'u'};
  parameter_1 = 's';
  auto &char_3 = char_1;
  auto char_4 = char_1;
  auto &char_5 = parameter_1;
  print("{}",
        char_4);
}
void run() {
  char char_1{'u'};
  char_1 = 's';
  auto &char_3 = char_1;
  auto char_4 = char_1;
  char char_5{'t'};
  char_4 = 'f';
  function(char_4, char_5);                        // f
                                                   // u

  auto &char_7 = char_5;
  auto char_8 = char_7;
  char char_9{'q'};
  auto char_10 = char_5;
  auto &char_11 = char_7;
  char char_12{'a'};
  char_5 = '.';
  function(char_10, char_3);                       // t
                                                   // u

  char char_14{'t'};
  std::swap(char_1, char_4);
  char_9 = 'k';
  auto &char_16 = char_7;
  std::swap(char_3, char_5);
  auto &char_17 = char_3;
  std::swap(char_17, char_12);
  char_4 = 'a';
  char char_19{'b'};
  char_19 = 'r';
  auto char_21 = char_7;
  char char_22{'e'};
```

```
  print("{}{}{}{}{}{}{}{}",                              // res.task
        char_19, char_22, char_10, char_12, char_14, char_17,
        char_16, char_9);
}
```

```
// Answer: futures.task
```

Solution 120

```
auto function(char &parameter_1, char parameter_2) {
  std::swap(parameter_1, parameter_2);
  char char_1{'r'};
  auto &char_2 = char_1;
  std::swap(parameter_2, char_2);
  parameter_1 = 'o';
  char char_4{'j'};
  print("{}",
        char_2);
}
void run() {
  char char_1{'c'};
  char_1 = 'v';
  char_1 = 'o';
  char char_4{'k'};
  char_1 = 'c';
  function(char_1, char_4);                              // c
  char_1 = 'r';
  char char_7{':'};
  char_4 = 'h';
  auto &char_9 = char_4;
  char char_10{'o'};
  function(char_9, char_10);                             // h
  char_4 = 'd';
  char char_12{':'};
  auto char_13 = char_12;
  char char_14{'t'};
  function(char_1, char_7);                              // r
  char_14 = 'g';
  std::swap(char_4, char_14);
  auto &char_16 = char_10;
  char_14 = 'f';
  auto char_18 = char_14;
  auto &char_19 = char_9;
```

```cpp
    std::swap(char_12, char_14);
    auto &char_20 = char_18;
    std::swap(char_9, char_19);
    auto char_21 = char_1;
    char char_22{'j'};
    char_9 = 'l';
    function(char_10, char_19);                          // o
    char char_24{'n'};
    char_20 = 'i';
    std::swap(char_1, char_18);
    char char_26{'f'};
    function(char_24, char_16);                          // n
    char_20 = 'r';
    function(char_24, char_26);                          // o
    auto char_28 = char_7;
    print("{}{}{}{}{}{}{}",                              // ::floor
        char_13, char_7, char_12, char_19, char_21, char_10,
        char_18);
}


// Answer: chrono::floor
```

Solution 121

```cpp
auto function(char &parameter_1, char &parameter_2) {
  parameter_2 = 'c';
  parameter_1 = 'q';
  char char_3{'l'};
  auto &char_4 = char_3;
  std::swap(char_3, parameter_2);
  auto &char_5 = parameter_2;
  print("{}",
      char_4);
}
void run() {
  char char_1{'c'};
  char char_2{'i'};
  char_1 = 'l';
  auto &char_4 = char_2;
  char_4 = 'a';
  print("{}",                                  // a
      char_4);
  auto char_6 = char_1;
```

```cpp
  char char_7{'m'};
  function(char_1, char_4);                              // c
  auto char_8 = char_7;
  char char_9{'l'};
  auto char_10 = char_9;
  char char_11{'a'};
  std::swap(char_4, char_10);
  char_9 = 't';
  char char_13{'u'};
  function(char_1, char_2);                              // c
  char char_14{'s'};
  auto char_15 = char_8;
  char char_16{'w'};
  char_14 = 'e';
  auto &char_18 = char_2;
  char char_19{'e'};
  char_6 = 'e';
  auto &char_21 = char_19;
  char_1 = 'u';
  auto &char_23 = char_13;
  print("{}{}{}{}{}{}{}",                                // umulate
        char_13, char_8, char_1, char_18, char_11, char_9,
        char_21);
}

// Answer: accumulate
```

Solution 122

```cpp
auto function(char &parameter_1, char &parameter_2) {
  parameter_2 = 'd';
  print("{}",
        parameter_1);
  char char_2{'b'};
  auto &char_3 = char_2;
  char char_4{'.'};
  auto &char_5 = parameter_2;
  print("{}{}",
        parameter_2, char_4);
}
void run() {
  char char_1{'d'};
  char char_2{'b'};
```

```cpp
    print("{}",                              // b
          char_2);
    char char_3{'a'};
    auto char_4 = char_1;
    std::swap(char_3, char_1);
    char char_5{'l'};
    auto char_6 = char_3;
    auto &char_7 = char_5;
    auto char_8 = char_5;
    std::swap(char_4, char_8);
    char char_9{'p'};
    auto char_10 = char_7;
    char char_11{'c'};
    function(char_1, char_2);                // a
                                             // d.

    auto &char_12 = char_9;
    char char_13{'k'};
    char_2 = 's';
    auto char_15 = char_8;
    auto &char_16 = char_1;
    auto char_17 = char_12;
    char_12 = 'o';
    char char_19{'c'};
    print("{}{}{}{}{}",                      // alloc
          char_16, char_10, char_7, char_12, char_19);
}


// Answer: bad.alloc
```

Solution 123

```cpp
auto function(char &parameter_1, char parameter_2) {
  char char_1{'g'};
  char char_2{'F'};
  char_1 = 'S';
  auto char_4 = char_2;
  auto &char_5 = char_1;
  char char_6{'T'};
  print("{}{}",
        char_4, char_6);
}
void run() {
  char char_1{'k'};
```

```cpp
  auto char_2 = char_1;
  char_1 = 'S';
  auto &char_4 = char_1;
  char_2 = 'E';
  char char_6{'T'};
  char_6 = 'u';
  auto char_8 = char_4;
  auto &char_9 = char_6;
  auto char_10 = char_8;
  char_10 = '-';
  auto char_12 = char_10;
  auto &char_13 = char_1;
  auto char_14 = char_4;
  auto &char_15 = char_8;
  char_9 = 'o';
  char char_17{'T'};
  char_8 = 'f';
  auto char_19 = char_12;
  function(char_17, char_14);                          // FT
  auto char_20 = char_1;
  char char_21{'T'};
  auto &char_22 = char_4;
  auto char_23 = char_21;
  char char_24{'i'};
  print("{}{}{}{}{}{}{}",                              // ST-TEST
        char_4, char_23, char_19, char_21, char_2, char_13,
        char_17);
}


// Answer: FTST-TEST
```

Solution 124

```cpp
auto function(char &parameter_1, char parameter_2) {
  parameter_1 = 'm';
  parameter_2 = 'e';
  std::swap(parameter_2, parameter_1);
  char char_3{'t'};
  print("{}{}",
        parameter_2, parameter_1);
  parameter_2 = 'w';
  print("{}",
        char_3);
```

```cpp
}
void run() {
  char char_1{'m'};
  auto char_2 = char_1;
  auto &char_3 = char_2;
  char char_4{'e'};
  std::swap(char_3, char_4);
  char_1 = 't';
  auto &char_6 = char_1;
  function(char_4, char_1);                        // me
                                                   // t

  char char_7{'x'};
  char_1 = 'h';
  char char_9{'s'};
  char_3 = 'e';
  auto &char_11 = char_6;
  auto char_12 = char_6;
  char char_13{'.'};
  char_12 = 'l';
  auto char_15 = char_13;
  std::swap(char_13, char_3);
  char char_16{'a'};
  auto char_17 = char_2;
  auto &char_18 = char_6;
  auto char_19 = char_2;
  char_7 = 'p';
  std::swap(char_16, char_3);
  char_4 = 'i';
  auto &char_22 = char_18;
  char char_23{'s'};
  auto char_24 = char_15;
  print("{}{}{}{}{}{}",                            // a.help
        char_3, char_24, char_18, char_13, char_12, char_7);
}


// Answer: meta.help
```

Solution 125

```cpp
auto function(char parameter_1, char &parameter_2) {
  std::swap(parameter_2, parameter_1);
  std::swap(parameter_2, parameter_1);
  parameter_1 = 'e';
  print("{}",
        parameter_1);
  char char_2{'.'};
  print("{}",
        char_2);
}
void run() {
  char char_1{'e'};
  char_1 = '.';
  auto &char_3 = char_1;
  char_1 = 'a';
  auto char_5 = char_3;
  auto &char_6 = char_3;
  char char_7{'r'};
  print("{}{}",                                    // ra
        char_7, char_3);
  auto &char_8 = char_7;
  char_5 = 'n';
  char char_10{'g'};
  char_3 = 'p';
  char char_12{'u'};
  char_6 = 'c';
  print("{}{}",                                    // ng
        char_5, char_10);
  auto char_14 = char_8;
  auto &char_15 = char_5;
  auto char_16 = char_5;
  char char_17{'y'};
  auto char_18 = char_1;
  auto &char_19 = char_17;
  char char_20{'r'};
  char_3 = 'o';
  char char_22{'b'};
  char_12 = 'm';
  char char_24{'w'};
  std::swap(char_24, char_18);
  char_7 = 'r';
```

```cpp
  function(char_3, char_16);                    // e
                                                // .

  auto &char_26 = char_19;
  char char_27{'e'};
  print("{}{}{}{}{}",                           // error
        char_27, char_14, char_8, char_6, char_20);
}

// Answer: range.error
```

Solution 126

```cpp
auto function(char parameter_1, char &parameter_2) {
  char char_1{'x'};
  parameter_2 = 'h';
  std::swap(parameter_1, parameter_2);
  auto char_3 = char_1;
  auto &char_4 = char_1;
  char char_5{'t'};
  print("{}{}",
        parameter_2, char_5);
}
void run() {
  char char_1{'j'};
  char_1 = 'y';
  char char_3{'l'};
  char_1 = 'a';
  char char_5{'t'};
  auto char_6 = char_5;
  char char_7{'.'};
  char_5 = 's';
  auto char_9 = char_1;
  char_6 = 'q';
  auto &char_11 = char_7;
  auto char_12 = char_6;
  char char_13{'n'};
  auto &char_14 = char_9;
  function(char_5, char_3);                     // st
  std::swap(char_12, char_1);
  auto &char_15 = char_1;
  char_14 = 'c';
  char char_17{'e'};
  auto char_18 = char_5;
```

```cpp
  char char_19{'y'};
  char_17 = 'l';
  char char_21{'l'};
  auto char_22 = char_13;
  char char_23{'e'};
  auto char_24 = char_13;
  char char_25{'k'};
  print("{}{}{}{}{}{}{}",                              // ack.syn
        char_12, char_14, char_25, char_7, char_3, char_19,
        char_13);
}

// Answer: stack.syn
```

Solution 127

```cpp
auto function(char &parameter_1, char parameter_2) {
  char char_1{'r'};
  parameter_2 = 'f';
  char char_3{'l'};
  auto &char_4 = parameter_1;
  std::swap(char_1, char_3);
  char_1 = 'e';
  print("{}{}",
        parameter_2, char_1);
}
void run() {
  char char_1{'r'};
  auto char_2 = char_1;
  char char_3{'l'};
  auto char_4 = char_2;
  char_1 = 'e';
  auto &char_6 = char_1;
  char char_7{'c'};
  function(char_1, char_2);                    // fe
  char_4 = 'q';
  char char_9{'l'};
  std::swap(char_7, char_6);
  char char_10{'g'};
  auto &char_11 = char_9;
  std::swap(char_11, char_9);
  auto char_12 = char_2;
  char_4 = 'a';
```

```cpp
    char char_14{'x'};
    auto char_15 = char_2;
    char_14 = 'e';
    char char_17{'b'};
    auto &char_18 = char_1;
    char_12 = 'q';
    char char_20{'x'};
    char_2 = 'e';
    auto &char_22 = char_7;
    char char_23{'t'};
    char_9 = 'p';
    char char_25{'y'};
    auto char_26 = char_7;
    auto &char_27 = char_20;
    print("{}{}{}{}{}{}{}{}{}{}{}",                 // clearexcept
          char_18, char_3, char_2, char_4, char_15, char_7,
          char_27, char_1, char_14, char_9, char_23);
}

// Answer: feclearexcept
```

Solution 128

```cpp
auto function(char &parameter_1, char &parameter_2) {
  std::swap(parameter_2, parameter_1);
  print("{}",
        parameter_1);
  parameter_1 = 'e';
  char char_2{'s'};
  auto char_3 = parameter_1;
  auto &char_4 = parameter_1;
  print("{}",
        parameter_2);
}
void run() {
  char char_1{'e'};
  auto char_2 = char_1;
  auto &char_3 = char_2;
  auto char_4 = char_3;
  char_2 = 'n';
  auto &char_6 = char_1;
  auto char_7 = char_3;
  char char_8{'n'};
```

```
  auto &char_9 = char_2;
  auto char_10 = char_4;
  char_10 = 'w';
  char char_12{'i'};
  function(char_2, char_12);                          // i
                                                      // n

  char char_13{'p'};
  char_9 = 'e';
  auto char_15 = char_4;
  auto &char_16 = char_15;
  char char_17{'v'};
  auto char_18 = char_10;
  auto &char_19 = char_2;
  char char_20{'s'};
  char_17 = 't';
  auto char_22 = char_3;
  char_15 = 'd';
  auto char_24 = char_22;
  function(char_2, char_16);                          // d
                                                      // e

  char_4 = 'd';
  char char_26{'u'};
  print("{}{}{}{}{}{}{}",                             // pendent
        char_13, char_2, char_8, char_4, char_1, char_12,
        char_17);
}

// Answer: independent
```